W9-AVB-784

Involving Hard-to-Reach Parents

Involving Hard-to-Reach Parents: Creating Family/ School Partnerships

Donald C. Lueder

ROWMAN & LITTLEFIELD EDUCATION

A division of

ROWMAN & LITTLEFIELD PUBLISHERS, INC.
Lanham • New York • Toronto • Plymouth, UK

Published by Rowman & Littlefield Education
A division of Rowman & Littlefield Publishers, Inc.
A wholly owned subsidary of The Rowman & Littlefield Publishing Group, Inc.
4501 Forbes Boulevard, Suite 200, Lanham, Maryland 20706
www.rowmaneducation.com

Estover Road
Plymouth PL6 7PY
United Kingdom

Copyright © 2011 by Donald C. Lueder

All rights reserved. No part of this book may be reproduced in any form or by any electronic or mechanical means, including information storage and retrieval systems, without written permission from the publisher, except by a reviewer who may quote passages in a review.

British Library Cataloguing in Publication Information Available

Library of Congress Cataloging-in-Publication Data

Lueder, Donald C.
  Involving hard-to-reach parents : creating family/school partnerships / Donald C. Lueder.
      p. cm.
  Includes bibliographical references and index.
  ISBN 978-1-61048-047-5 (cloth : alk. paper) — ISBN 978-1-61048-048-2 (pbk.) — ISBN 978-1-61048-049-9 (electronic)
  1. Home and school—United States.   2. Education—Parent participation—United States.   3. Community and school—United States.   4. School improvement programs—United States.   I. Title.
  LC225.3.L85 2011
  371.19'2—dc22   2010035716

Printed in the United States of America

♾ ™ The paper used in this publication meets the minimum requirements of American National Standard for Information Sciences—Permanence of Paper for Printed Library Materials, ANSI/NISO Z39.48-1992.

To my wife, Jan,
who was my partner in this endeavor
at home and at school

Contents

Prologue

In the late 1990s, parent involvement was one of the buzzwords being bantered around by educators, policy makers, and legislators. Now, over 10 years later, the lack of involvement by some parents in the education of their children is still a major issue.

While many parents are involved, some families are "missing in action." *Involving Hard-to-Reach Parents: Creating Family/School Partnerships* presents a comprehensive strategy for reaching out to help the missing families get involved. This book is different from other parent involvement publications because it presents, in practical terms, ways to develop and establish collaborative relationships with parents, especially those that are underserved.

Involving Hard-to-Reach Parents is about change—change that can help many children to get the help and support they need to be successful. The book is for anyone who wants to reach out and work with *all* families.

The notion of "reaching out" is essential. Without making this effort, it is unlikely that many families will be fully involved in the education of their children. As a result, many children will not reach their potential.

The Self-Renewing Partnership Model presented in the book is a comprehensive paradigm for designing and implementing family/school partnership programs with all families. The model contains four Partnership Intervention Strategies: connecting, communicating, coordinating, and coaching. These intervention strategies are hierarchal in nature. That is, one builds upon the other with coaching being the highest level. An array of best practices (programs, events, and activities) are presented that can be used to implement the various Partnership Intervention Strategies.

Chapter 1

Introduction: the Case of the Missing Families

THE DILEMMA

Educators are faced with a frustrating two-pronged dilemma. First, superintendents, principals, and teachers are finding it exceedingly difficult, if not impossible, to reach many students in a meaningful way because they are coming to school with inadequate basic skills and knowledge. Further, these deficiencies are often accompanied with self-defeating attitudes. Second, educators have not found a way to gain the necessary support from the families to help avoid or solve these problems.

The flames of the dilemma are fanned by increasing social pressures resulting from the effects of such things as: unemployment, divorce, lack of health care, drug and alcohol abuse, violence, teenage pregnancy, and children with special needs. Unfortunately, as the pressures have increased, the availability of resources has decreased. Simply put, the schools find themselves caught in a bind.

While educators generally believe more parent involvement is needed, they are not sure how to reach many of the families. Rutherford (1995) emphasizes this point when he states, "How to involve these parents [families] productively remains an open question, especially since few teachers and administrators have received training in working with parents [families]"(p. 6).

In the past, superintendents, principals, curriculum coordinators, project directors, and teachers have been forced to use their intuition in a "hit-or-miss" fashion when they developed parent involvement programs. They implemented several traditional activities and events hoping one of them would work. They had no option since there was no conceptual framework to follow. As a result, sometimes their efforts were successful, and other times they were

1

not. Kressley (2008) suggests that current education policy often results in what she calls "random acts of family involvement."

Milbrey McLaughlin, of Stanford University, argues that "The level of parent involvement at school is not determined by parent interest or apathy. The level of parent involvement is determined by whether or not appropriate strategies and structures are in place to facilitate the participation of parents." In an effort to respond to the dilemma, a model for involving all families in the education of their children, both at school and home, has been developed.

The Self-Renewing Partnership Model is a comprehensive method for designing and implementing partnerships between the families and the school. With this paradigm, the school reaches out to the families to establish collaborative relationships. This is radically different from the traditional parent involvement approach described in the next section.

Parents or Families?

Often the word "families" is used in place of "parents," when referring to the significant others who are the child's caregiver and provider. I believe the new terminology more accurately reflexes the realities of today's families, and the complexities of being involved in the child's education.

In many families, instead of the biological parent, or in addition to, grandmothers, grandfathers, aunts, uncles, brothers, sisters, friends, etc., are the individuals impacting directly on the child's educational and social development. Therefore, terms like "family involvement, family resource center, and family/school coordinator" have emerged to indicate the new roles and responsibilities.

However, I also believe the words "parents" and "parenting" are generally understood and accepted. Therefore, these terms are used interchangeably with "family" to describe some of the programs and activities. No matter what terminology is used, it is important to recognize and acknowledge that many different family members may be serving in the various roles that are encompassed in the difficult task of parenting.

The Traditional Parent Involvement Approach

Typically, parent involvement programs have been essentially single-dimensional, with family resources flowing into the school for the purpose of supporting the school's curriculum, programs, and activities. The families provide time, money, and expertise to help their children.

Consequently, it's not surprising that when superintendents, principals, teachers, and parents are asked to give examples of parent involvement, their answers are very similar. They cite such activities as serving as volunteers and chaperones; working on fundraising drives; attending athletic, music, and theater events; and participating in PTO meetings, open houses, and parent/teacher conferences. These programs and activities reflect the traditional "families supporting the school" parent involvement approach.

This approach is firmly ingrained in most school cultures. My wife and I can personally relate to this. Over the years, we have sold dozens of hot dogs and gallons of soft drinks at football games, and have attended countless number of band concerts, soccer matches, dance recitals, and plays. We have met with teachers, principals, and guidance counselors.

Most of us are intimately familiar with these activities. I am sure you can provide examples of your involvement and elaborate on your adventures. You would probably say you would gladly do it all again, and would argue that this kind of participation is very important to the child and the school.

All of this is true. However, the "families supporting the school" approach is only one aspect of being involved in the education of the child and does not do the job by itself. The traditional parent involvement approach suffers from serious limitations. If schools and communities continue to focus only on this approach, many families will not be involved, and their children will not receive the support and help they desperately need.

The Case of the Missing Families: a Systemic Problem

Usually, even in the best of situations, there is only a small group of families that are actively involved in the school. With schools that report they have great support from the parents, the percentage of families involved in the different events and activities usually hovers around 25 percent.

Having these parents being so involved has both its pluses and minuses. On the plus side, these are the families that always respond when there are special needs. These are the parents who will help to develop the partnerships. However, often these families are perceived by other families as "controlling" the school, a perception that can keep some parents away.

These characteristics are indicators of the benefits and limitations of the traditional parent involvement approach. While it is great to have a group of families that you can depend upon to help and support the school, this kind of involvement does not solve the dilemma described earlier.

The many family members who are not actively involved at school are a concern, but their absence is symptomatic of a much larger problem. I believe the major parent involvement issue facing this country is that many parents are not engaged in the education of their children at home. It is this group of "missing families" that needs attention. That is, the focus should be on the involvement in the home and the school.

Although I do not have empirical evidence to support my claim, my contention is that the family's involvement with the school is an extension, or outgrowth, of the family's involvement in the home. My belief is that being involved with the child's education at home is a prerequisite for being involved at school.

Because parental involvement in the home is fundamental, it is understandable why research studies show that the parents' involvement in the home has a greater impact on the academic and social development of the child than their involvement with the school. Consequently, involving the "missing families" with the child's education in the home is essential.

To achieve this, the schools must use a new approach. Currently, most calls for more parent involvement follow the traditional approach, concentrating mainly on ways to get the families to support the school. However, in order to solve the dilemma stated earlier, parent involvement programs must focus on increasing the families' involvement in the home *and* at school.

The Self-Renewing Partnership Model

The Self-Renewing Partnership Model presented here is a method for reaching and involving the "missing families" by creating partnerships between the family and school. The goal of the partnerships is to create "learning communities" where families and schools collaborate to provide the best possible educational opportunities and environments for the children. The nature and function of family/school partnerships are described and discussed in Chapter 3.

As mentioned, the Self-Renewing Partnership Model requires a shift in the way we have traditionally conceptualized the notion of parent involvement as it introduces a new outreach dimension for working with the parents. We can no longer think of parent involvement only as family members working with and supporting the school, the school must also work with and support the families.

Being involved in the child's education at home and at school is a complex task, and getting the families to be partners with the school can be difficult. Usually, many barriers keep some families and the school apart, thus making them "hard to reach." The school must work to overcome these obstacles. (The barriers are described in Chapter 4.)

The Self-Renewing Partnership Model has two dimensions that interact with each other: "energy-in" and "energy-out." The "energy-in" dimension expands on the traditional "families supporting the school" approach. The dimension is described as "energy-in" because the family's resources (time, money, and expertise) are directed at the school and at the child.

There are eight different roles the families have to play to be fully involved in the academic and social development of the children in the home and at school. These roles are called Parent Partner Roles. Some of the roles are directed at the school and others at the child. The Parent Partner Roles include: nurturer, communicator, teacher, supporter, learner, advisor, advocator, and collaborator. The Parent Partner Roles are described and discussed in the next chapter.

The "energy-out" dimension is designed to reach out and engage the families. This dimension includes four Partnership Intervention Strategies. It is this dimension that makes the Self-Renewing Partnership Model unique. The use of resources to reach out to the families is a new "direction" for involving parents. The Partnership Intervention Strategies are used to create collaborative relationships and enhance the families' willingness and ability to play the Parent Partner Roles. The four strategies are: connecting, communicating, coordinating, and coaching. The intervention strategies are progressive in nature and build on each other, coaching being the highest level. The strategies are implemented sequentially. First, the Connecting Strategy is employed to break down the barriers between the families and the school. The Communicating Strategy is then used to establish a two-way communication flow. The Coordinating Strategy is implemented to get school and community resources to the needy families. Finally, the Coaching Strategy is used to enhance the family's ability and capacity to play their Parent Partner Roles. Whether all of the interventions are needed, or which one is emphasized, depends upon the families' conditions and level of involvement.

A separate chapter is devoted to each Partnership Intervention Strategy (chapters 6, 7, 8, and 9). Each chapter includes best practices (activities, events, and programs) for implementing each strategy. The best practices are some that I have used and some have been gathered from successful partnership programs in the United States and Europe.

SUMMARY

Using school resources to reach out to the families is not the norm. However, I believe this must to be done to connect with and involve the "missing families." Even with limited resources, schools must be willing to implement strategies to reach and work with the hard-to-reach parents. It is vital that we involve all of the parents since the success and happiness of our children is at stake. Building partnerships between the families and schools is what parental involvement should be about. By using the Self-Renewing Partnership Model to create family/school partnerships with all parents, especially the underserved, the case of the "missing" families can be solved.

Chapter 2

Fully Involved Families: the Goal

Reaching out and helping all parents, or surrogates, to be involved in the educational and social development of their children is the major focus of this book. The Self-Renewing Partnership Model has been developed to help schools and communities to accomplish this goal by creating partnerships between the families and school. The model uses intervention strategies to reach the parents and help them be fully involved in their children's education. But, what does it mean to be "fully involved?"

The concept parental involvement held by many people is very narrow because it is based solely on the traditional "families supporting the school" approach. Being "fully involved," on the other hand, means that the parents are engaged in the child's education in the home and at school. Partnership programs are based on this broader view.

To better understand the characteristics of the fully involved family, the specific roles that parents must be willing and able to play to be partners have been identified and are described in this chapter. The Parent Partner Roles include: nurturer, communicator, teacher, supporter, learner, advisor, advocator, and collaborator. Again, the word "parent" here refers to any family member or surrogate who is assuming the parenting roles.

Not surprisingly, many family members have difficulty knowing how and when to play the Parent Partner Roles, which helps explain why there are so many "missing families." Therefore, the function of the Coaching Strategy in the proposed model is to help the families to enhance their skills and knowledge to play the Parent Partner Roles.

PARENT INVOLVEMENT: WHAT IS IT?

It has been said, "If there is lots of agreement about the solution to a problem, then the problem must not be understood very well." This may be the case with the parent involvement issue. Calls for more involvement by the families are coming from many arenas across the nation (and the world, for that matter) and from leaders in corporations, legislatures, colleges of education, universities, public schools, and communities. However, many of those arguing for more involvement appear not to know or understand what it is they are seeking.

Anyone reading this would agree that getting more parents involved is a good idea, but we might not agree on the desired outcomes of the involvement. We need to be clear about what outcomes we want from the partnerships between families and schools. As the adage points out, "It is hard to get lost if you don't know where you are going." That is, we need to know where we want to go with the involvement.

As stated in the beginning of this chapter, I believe too many people are operating solely from the traditional "families supporting the school" approach without considering how parents influence their children both at school and in the home. As we plan partnership programs, we have to consider the many ways parents need to be involved in the child's education.

An Exercise

The responses from a simple exercise provide good indicators of the desired outcomes of parental involvement. When thinking about this issue, I asked myself, "What are the things that families provide when they are fully involved in the academic and social development of their children?" I posed this question, in a slightly different way, to groups of students, educators, and community leaders across the United States. These people were graduate students of mine, workshop participants, or members of the audience at some of my presentations. As I worked with these groups, I asked them to respond to the question, "What did your family provide you and instill in you that helped you get where you are today?"

Figure 2.1 is a summary of their responses. However, before looking at the answers, ask yourself the same question. List your outcomes on paper, or in your mind, and compare them with the answers presented in Figure 2.1.

The outcomes listed in Figure 2.1 are impressive. Hopefully, you can identify with many or most of them. If you can, it is likely that you feel your family was involved.

Responses to the question: "What did your family provide you and instill in you that helped you get where you are today?"

Provided
- love and nurturing
- day-to-day necessities
- stable and safe environment
- financial support
- psychological support and encouragement
- advice and guidance
- understanding, caring, and respect
- monitoring and supervision
- discipline and structure
- exposure to new experiences and opportunities
- a good learning environment

Instilled
- basic skills and knowledge
- problem-solving skills
- a questioning of why and why not
- high expectations and standards
- strong value system (e.g., responsibility, independence, perseverance)
- respect for others and yourself
- belief that education is important
- work ethic
- belief in yourself
- sense of security

Figure 2.1   A Summary of Desired Outcomes of Parental Involvement.

Obviously, if all children received the kind of support from their families that is listed in Figure 2.1, we would not be as concerned about getting more parents involved. Unfortunately, this is not the case. Many children are not the beneficiaries of this kind of involvement.

To help solve the "case of the missing families," we have to find a way to reduce the discrepancy between the amount and kind of support provided by many of the families, and the amount and kind of support that is needed for the children to be successful. The Self-Renewing Partnership Model, presented in chapter 5, is a method for reducing the discrepancy and increasing the involvement of parents, especially the "hard to reach."

PARENT PARTNER ROLES

Parent Partner Roles, as stated before, are the roles that family members must be willing and able to play in order to be fully involved in the educational and social development of their children. The eight roles are: nurturer, communicator, teacher, supporter, learner, advisor, advocator, and collaborator. Some of the roles are directed at the child, some at the school, and some at both the child and the school.

Existing research greatly influenced me as I delineated the roles the families needed to be able to play to be fully involved partners. For example, Anne Henderson, Carl Marburger, and Theodora Ooms's 1986 book *Beyond the Bake Sale* challenged the traditional view of parent involvement. They describe five basic parent involvement roles: partners, collaborators and problem solvers, audience, supporters, and advisors, and/or codecision-makers. These ideas are enhanced in the 2007 edition of *Beyond the Bake Sale* by Henderson, Mapp, Johnson, and Don Davies.

Janet Chrispeels (1988, 1992) emphasizes the reciprocal nature of the home and the school roles. Her seven roles are cocommunicators, cosupporters, colearners, coteachers, and coadvisors, codecision-makers, and coadvocates.

Joyce Epstein (1987, 1992) formulated a framework of six major types of involvement in a family/school partnership. She now refers to the framework as "six types of caring" (Epstein, et al. 2009). The terminology and content indicates the realities of today's family structures, and emphasizes the notion that communities should be partners in the education of the children. The six types are parenting, communicating, volunteering, learning at home, decision-making, and collaborating with community.

Epstein's framework is widely used by many schools when developing their parent involvement programs. The Self-Renewing Partnership Model presented in the next chapter (Chapter 3) can be used to implement Epstein's framework.

In addition to the research, I used data from successful parent involvement programs and the responses from the previously discussed question: "What did your family provide you and instill in you that helped you get where you are today?"

The Parent Partner Roles are used as a guide when preparing to coach the parents. By knowing and understanding these roles educators can employ the best practices more effectively. That is, it is much easier to decide which intervention strategies to use when you know what outcomes you want to achieve. (Best practices for coaching the parents are presented in chapter 9.)

The eight Parent Partner Roles below evolved from these various sources:

Nurturer (child-directed): The function of the Nurturer Role is to provide an appropriate environment where the child will flourish physically, psychologically, and emotionally.

Communicator (child- and school-directed): The function of the Communicator Role is to establish and maintain effective two-way communication flows with the child and the school.

Teacher (child-directed): The function of the Teacher Role is to assist with the child's moral, intellectual, emotional, and social development.

Supporter (child- and school-directed): The function of the Supporter Role is to be actively supportive of the child's at-school learning activities and the school's curriculum and other programs.

Learner (child-directed): The function of the Learner Role is to obtain new skills and knowledge that will help directly and indirectly with the child's educational and social development.

Advisor (child-directed): The function of the Advisor Role is to wisely counsel and advise the child concerning his or her personal and educational issues.

Advocator (child- and school-directed): The function of the Advocator Role is to effectively and actively mediate and negotiate for the child.

Collaborator: The function of the Collaborator Role is to work effectively with the school and community to help study issues, solve problems, make decisions, and develop policy.

Figure 2.2   Parent Partner Roles

THE PROGRESSIVE NATURE OF THE PARENT PARTNER ROLES

The Parent Partner Roles are hierarchical and progressive. That is, the roles build upon one another. Thus, the role behaviors range from the more basic and fundamental (nurturer, communicator, teacher, and supporter) to the more specialized (advisor, advocator, and collaborator). All the roles are essential, as the "lower" order roles provide the foundation for the other "higher" level roles. Roles such as advisor, advocator, and collaborator cannot be played unless the parents are able to play the lower-level roles effectively. For example, to be a good advisor, a parent must know what is going on in the child's life in school (Communicator Role) and have established a learning environment in the home (Nurturer Role).

The family members are expected to play the lower-level roles all the time, and only assume some of the high-level roles, such as advocator and advisor when the need arises. Although the higher-level roles are played less frequently, the parents must be prepared to assume them at the appropriate times. For example, family members need to be skilled in such areas as mediation, problem-solving, advising, and conflict resolution to play the higher-order roles.

In the following sections, the eight Parent Partner Roles are described and discussed, including examples of expectations and activities for each.

Nurturer Role (Child-Directed)

The function of the Nurturer Role is to provide an appropriate environment where the child will flourish physically, psychologically, and emotionally. As such, the Nurturer Role is child-directed, concerned with maintaining positive learning conditions at home and the child's overall health, shelter, safety, and behavior. The outcomes from this role form the foundation on which the Parent Partner Roles are played.

Expectations Associated with the Nurturer Role

- offering love, praise, and encouragement
- being understanding, caring, and respectful
- providing day-to-day necessities
- giving overall financial support
- establishing a stable and safe environment and a sense of security
- instilling a belief that education is important
- modeling a work ethic
- supporting the child's education by providing an appropriate learning environment

Examples of Activities Associated with the Nurturer Role

- establishing a daily family routine
- providing school supplies and equipment, medical examinations, vaccinations, and so on
- regulating the use of television, Internet, telephones (voice and texting), and video games including time and content
- scheduling and monitoring daily homework times

- responding to school's request for registration forms, schedules, report card signatures, permission slips, and other information
- monitoring the child's in-school attendance and behavior and out-of-school activities

Communicator Role (Child- and School-Directed)

The function of the Communicator Role is to establish and maintain an effective two-way communication flow with the child and the school. As such, the Communicator Role is intertwined with all of the other Parent Partner Roles. The importance of being a good communicator has long been recognized by most scholars in the field.

The Communicator Role is a complex lower-order role because it encompasses three major communication flows: between the family and the child, the family and the school, and the child and the school, while building on the Nurturer Role.

Although this role centers on the parents, we must not forget that in a partnership, the school must also communicate effectively with the family and the child. (Programs, activities, and events for helping the school to communicate effectively with the parents are presented in chapter 7.)

Expectations Associated with the Communicator Role

- communicating and listening effectively and accurately
- communicating with understanding, empathy and high regard

Examples of Activities Associated with the Communicator Role

Child-Directed

- communicating with the child about successes in school and home
- communicating with the child about problems and concerns
- communicating to the child the ways you can support him or her in programs and activities

School-Directed

- communicating with the school about what is going on in the child's school life
- maintaining continuous communication with the school about how you can support the child

- dialoguing with the school about the child's progress, strengths, and weaknesses
- participating in productive parent/teacher or parent/student/teacher conferences
- responding promptly and effectively to letters and phone calls from school
- making timely and appropriate requests for information, assistance, and advice
- visiting the school regularly to talk with teachers, counselors, and principals
- participating in informal meetings with principal and/or teachers

Teacher Role (Child-Directed)

The function of the Teacher Role is to assist with the child's moral, intellectual, emotional, and social development. Few would disagree with the statement that, "The parent is the child's first teacher, and possibly, the child's most important teacher." The effect the family has on the child, especially in the early years, is dramatic and fundamental. It is essential, therefore, that the parents are able to teach the child in the home. However, many families need help to enhance their ability to perform this most important role.

Expectations Associated with the Teacher Role

- instilling in the child a strong sense of ethics, standards, and high expectations
- exposing the child to positive values and character traits, such as respect, responsibility, and integrity
- teaching basic skills and knowledge
- initiating learning activities or responding to the child's requests for help
- developing in the child a belief in himself or herself

Examples of Activities Associated with the Teacher Role

- reading to the child, reading together, and/or making sure the child reads at home
- working with the child on math, problem-solving, and reasoning skills in the home during daily tasks and on family trips
- working with the child's teachers to coordinate classroom work with home-based learning activities
- exposing the child to various cultural, career, scientific, and historic sites, events, and programs

Supporter Role (Child- and School-Directed)

The function of the Supporter Role is to be actively supportive of the child's at-school learning activities and the school's overall curriculum and other programs. While the Supporter Role is both school- and child-directed, it is set in the context of being supportive in the school environment. Sometimes, the family's involvement is a combination of support for the child and the school. Playing the Supporter Role at school can be very active, for example, participating in open houses, volunteering, chaperoning, and so on, or more passive, such as, attending basketball games, band concerts, play, and so on, and visiting student art exhibits, science fairs, and so forth.

Expectations Associated with the Supporter Role

- supporting the child's participation in school activities, programs, and events
- providing support to the school for its curriculum, programs, activities, and events

Examples of Activities Associated with the Supporter Role

Child-Directed

- attending school concerts, plays, award assemblies, sport events, and other productions
- visiting student art exhibits, science fairs, and other demonstrations
- participating in daughter or son dinners and dances, senior teas, ethnic suppers, and so on
- participating in classroom events, open houses, and PTA/PTO programs

School-Directed

- assisting teachers, administrators, and children in classrooms, or in other areas of the school
- participating in booster clubs and fund-raisers
- chaperoning field trips and dances
- organizing and conduct campus clean-ups and beautification projects

Learner Role (Child-Directed)

The function of the Learner Role is to obtain new skills and knowledge that will help directly and indirectly with the child's educational and social development. Parenting is a difficult task, therefore, it is important that the family members continually obtain new skills and knowledge. Parenting and learning are lifelong experiences. While the outcomes of the learning will benefit the child, new skills and knowledge also help the parents with their own development, growth, and life satisfaction.

Expectations Associated with the Learner Role

- enhancing skills and knowledge related to the parent partner roles
- obtaining knowledge and skills to enhance individual and family quality of life

Examples of Activities Associated with the Learner Role

- enrolling in parent education classes, continuing and adult education programs, and family center classes to improve general knowledge and skills in such areas as math, language, geography, educational issues, reading, and literature
- reading and studying materials on such topics as school curriculum and activities, basic skill development, family and student rights, college preparation, and dropout prevention
- participating in support groups and parent education workshops that focus on such topics as child development, parenting skills, alcohol and drug abuse, and teenage pregnancy
- learning about school board policies, and school rules and regulations

Advisor Role (Child-Directed)

The function of the Advisor Role is to wisely counsel and advise the child concerning his or her personal and educational situation. Since this is a higher-order Parent Partner Role, the parents must be able to play the lower-order roles first. For example, the family members and children need to be able to communicate with each other and have a trusting relationship. The parents need to truly *advise,* rather than telling the children what to do.

Expectations Associated with the Advisor Role

- being able to listen to the child's problems and concerns
- establishing a helping relationship with the child
- offering advice, and counseling in an appropriate way

Examples of Activities Associated with the Advisor Role

- helping with personal concerns and problems
- assisting with curriculum and program issues
- advising about potential career paths and opportunities
- being familiar with the contents of the child's student records
- knowing and understanding the standardized testing process

Advocator Role (Child- and School-Directed)

The function of the Advocator Role is to effectively and actively mediate and negotiate for the child. Like the Supporter Role, the Advocator Role is generally played in the school environment. As the Advocator Role is a higher-order role, the parents need to possess specific skills and knowledge to effectively play the role. In addition, they also need to be good communicators and supporters.

Expectations Associated with the Advocator Role

- being available to mediate and advocate for the child when needed
- being knowledgeable of school policy, curriculum, programs, and activities

Examples of Activities Associated with the Advocator Role

- helping to resolve conflicts, concerns, and problems related to curriculum, programs, and activities
- reinforcing the proper enforcement of family and student rights
- monitoring the application of school policies and practices
- requesting copies of written school and school district policies
- advocating for curricular and operational policy and procedural reform

Collaborator Role (School-Directed)

The function of the Collaborator Role is to work effectively with the school to help study issues, solve problems, make decisions, and develop policy. The term "collaborator" was chosen because it expresses the nature of the working relationship between the family and the school. Being a collaborator requires higher-order skills and knowledge. This role is at the top of the hierarchy, building on all of the other Parent Partner Roles. Realistically, many family members will not play this role, however; if they chose to do so, they must be properly prepared.

Expectations Associated with the Collaborator Role

- entering into a collegial relationship with the school
- possessing the skills and knowledge to help with problem-solving, program development, curriculum design, policy decisions, and so on

Examples of Activities Associated with the Collaborator Role

- participating in school improvement and community councils, school planning and management teams, special projects, and school committees where families have equal status with professionals and representatives from the community
- assisting in reducing educational barriers
- monitoring health, library, and cultural services to make sure they are easily accessible to the school and neighborhood
- attending school board meetings
- serving on the school board and city council
- participating in (or organizing) family-family organizations
- appealing local school and school system decisions that are questionable or not understood
- being involved in curriculum activities
- influencing school policy
- participating on committees that focus on such issues as maintaining a safe environment in and around the campus, bus safety, upgrading and beautifying the school building and grounds, and establishing and maintaining high standards and expectations, quality programs, and extracurricular options

SUMMARY

The Parent Partner Roles are the eight roles that the parents or family members must be prepared to assume if they are to be fully involved in the education of their children. These progressive roles are separate, but interrelated aspects of the complicated and elusive act of parenting. Because the roles build upon one another, on occasion, the family members play many roles during a particular event or activity. For example, at a conference between a parent and a teacher, the parent must be prepared to play the roles of communicator, supporter, learner, and advocator. Consequently, the parent needs the skills and knowledge to be ready and willing to play the right role at the right time.

Learning to parent is an ongoing process. Just when you think you are "on top of your game," something occurs that causes you to wonder if you know anything at all about parenting. Fortunately, or unfortunately, this is the reality of being a parent, and this is why we all need help at times. The intent of the Coaching Strategy is to provide this help and allow parents to be fully involved in the education of the children.

By creating partnerships between the families and school, we can provide enriching learning and supportive environments for the children in the home and at school. The nature and function of family/school partnerships are discussed in the next chapter.

Chapter 3

Family/School Partnerships: a Solution

Family/school partnerships are fertile environments for collaboration and providing families with ideal settings for enhancing and playing their Parent Partner Roles. The notion of a partnership is that *everyone* is responsible for the education of the children, and by working together, all children will have a better chance to be successful.

With partnerships, the resources, or "energies," of the various stakeholders are aligned so everyone is making a contribution to the common goal of learning. However, for this to happen requires a concerted, sustained, collaborative effort. Family/school partnerships need to be planned, formed, and cultivated. This chapter explains the nature and function of family/school partnerships, and how these relationships benefit not only the children, but also all parties involved.

In chapter 5, a comprehensive model for designing and building the partnerships is presented. Later chapters, in turn, describe and discuss the strategies for implementing the model. But the first step in planning a partnership program is to have a common understanding of what a family/school partnership really is.

WHAT IS A FAMILY/SCHOOL PARTNERSHIP?

A family/school partnership is a collaborative relationship between the family and school designed primarily to produce positive educational and social effects on the child, while being mutually beneficial to all other parties involved.

As the definition suggests, the concept of partnerships between the family and school is more far-reaching and complex than such interactions as "home/school relations" or "family/school cooperation." These latter terms are rather general and informal, while the idea of a "partnership" connotes a more defined coalition or alliance and suggests a formal, or informal, "contract" between the family and school. The partnership philosophy of collaboration and cooperation between all parties is more comprehensive than the underpinnings of the traditional parent involvement approach. As indicated earlier, parent involvement programs have typically focused primarily on the family's involvement at school with the intent of gaining support for the school's curriculum, activities, and programs, such as volunteer activities, PTA/PTOs, open houses, and so on.

Family/school partnerships, on the other hand, have a much broader focus, encompassing the families' and the school's involvement in the child's education both at school and in the home.

The partnerships should not be seen as ends in themselves, but as a means for the families and school to work together to enhance the academic and social growth of children. Thus, the partnerships are more of a process based on a collaborative and helping attitude, and belief system than a product. They are environments for people to help each other, so they can help the children.

A family/school partnership offers the parties involved the opportunity to effectively play their individual roles and fulfill their responsibilities. As such, they are small learning communities where the families and school can concentrate on the sources of the educational and social problems, rather than merely symptoms. Problems such as low achievement, poor attendance, dropouts, misbehavior, teenage pregnancy, and drug abuse are symptoms of more deeply rooted social and family issues like poverty, dysfunctional family relationships, lack of health care, and poor parenting skills and knowledge.

I believe that most social problems will ultimately be solved through education. Therefore, it is imperative that we work together on doing the right things in the right way.

Creating partnerships with families is a complex task, especially with the hard-to-reach parents. Those seeking more involvement by these parents must recognize it will take a long-term comprehensive effort by the school for this to happen.

When planning a family/school partnership program, therefore, it should be kept in mind that formation of collaborative relationships usually requires changes in school and family cultures. A change in attitude is often needed as well. This doesn't happen all at once. Someone asked me one time, "How long do we have to work to involve the parents?" I answered, "Forever!"

Collaboration is the concept that underlies a family/school partnership. Webster defines collaboration as: "to work jointly with others." Roget's *Thesaurus* lists terms such as cooperation, willingness, joint effort, synergy, and teamwork when referring to collaboration. However, even these words do not fully describe the close working relationships that are characteristic of this kind of partnership. The relationships in a family/school partnership are built on trust, mutual regard, caring, and shared beliefs. Therefore, they are usually deep and complex. The collaborative relationships are formed on the assumption that education is a shared responsibility and that all partners are equal players. "Equal," in this case, means that each partner contributes in major ways to the success of young people, and that everyone has a say in determining the path to the common goal of learning.

While education is still considered primarily to be the domain of the school, in a partnership, it is recognized that the family possesses unique strengths, resources, and expertise that can have a positive impact on the learning process.

One of the goals of the Self-Renewing Partnership Model is to increase the family members' ability and willingness to play their Parent Partner Roles. Although some parents may need help, and even seek help, they do not want to feel they are being fixed.

Even the most distressed families have strengths and a sense of pride. Efforts should be made not to patronize or demean family members as we work to increase their involvement and to increase their capacities to be partners. This is why the intervention strategy for helping the families to enhance their skills and knowledge is called "coaching."

Educational excellence is a hollow goal if it does not promise and expect equity. Until recently, the concern for equity in education has been taking second place to the concern for educational excellence. You cannot have excellence if it is not for everyone.

Years ago, a family education program forcefully expressed the goal of equality and independence, rather than codependency, in its vision statement. Their guiding philosophy was, "If you have come here to help me, you are wasting your time. If you came because your liberation is bound up with mine, then let us work together." (Rioux & Berla, 1993, p. 314) What a great philosophy.

BUILDING ON FAMILY STRENGTHS

Involving the families in the learning process, especially in the home, makes perfect sense since more than 80 percent of a student's time is spent out of school. Families have a great untapped capacity to work with their children at home in many ways, as well as to assist the schools with their programs and activities.

A major strength is that the parent (or surrogate) is the child's first teacher, which provides for an almost unlimited opportunity to teach, model, and guide. Families know their children better than anyone else, having intimate knowledge of their needs, skills, and talents. Most families also have a keen interest in their children's future and want them to succeed; as a result, they want to be involved in the education of their children.

Efforts to engage the families should focus on their strengths, not their weaknesses. Unfortunately, when attempts have been made to involve the families, at times, the focus has been on the latter. Although many families have problems, the school must not use a deficit approach when working with them. Metaphorically, we must concentrate on the doughnut, not the hole.

We need to work with the faculty and staff to alter any preconceptions they might have about the inadequacies of parents. For example, any idea of "them against us" must be dispelled and replaced with a win-win attitude to ensure that the teachers and families benefit from the partnerships. As a result, when developing a partnership program, those involved need to believe that:

- the probability of higher student achievement, as well as more excitement and joy in the classroom and at home, is greater when this kind of learning community is created.
- even though the child is central to the relationship, engaging the families in the education of their children will not only help the children, but also the family and school as well.
- when the families work collaboratively with the school, everyone should find their roles less stressful, more productive and more rewarding. There will be fewer conflicts and problems.

PREVENTION RATHER THAN THE CURE

Many of the benefits from the partnerships are visible and respond directly to a need, for example, workshops, food pantries, and tutoring. However, most of the benefits for the teachers and principals are more indirect and preventive in nature, including reduced stress, increased morale, and greater feelings of accomplishment. Throughout, the idea is that by having a good working relationship between the family and school, fewer problems will arise. And if problems do arise, they will be more easily solved and addressed.

As the auto mechanic said on an old television ad for oil filters, "Pay me now, or pay me later." If we do not reach out and connect with all families to solve some of the problems now and help the children, we will be faced with even bigger problems later. As a result, it will take some selling for teachers, principals, and counselors to buy into a "pay now, so you won't have to pay later" concept. This is not easy because our culture tends to want immediate results: along with a 100 percent guarantee. The Connecting Strategy chapter includes best practices to prepare the faculty and staff for the partnerships.

A Word about Empowerment:

All teachers want to help the kids, but they also would like some help for themselves. Teachers and principals need to feel they are more effective, productive, happier, and less stressed when the families are working closely with the school (naturally, you would hope the families feel this way as well).

As you seek to empower parents, you also need to provide an opportunity for teachers to increase their control and decision-making over events and conditions of their work life. Teachers need to feel supported and empowered to reach out to the families. Usually, they are not anxious to add this responsibility unless they feel they are seen as responsible by the principal.

Most teachers are not willing to share decision-making with the parents unless they feel they have authority to make decisions themselves. Schools operating successful partnership programs and school improvement projects usually have faculties and staffs that feel strong, secure, and empowered to make important decisions about their work and personal life. They are eager for more information and resources that would help them to enhance the academic and social development of the children.

A downside to this is that all too often as more responsibilities are added to the teachers' already overloaded schedules, nothing is taken away. As one tired teacher remarked, "I'm not sure that I can stand much more empowerment."

We need to be cognizant of the additional loads that are being placed on the faculty and staff to prevent them from becoming overwhelmed. If involving the families just means more work for the teachers, it is unlikely that the partnership will flourish. Best practices need to be implemented to free up the teachers and staff to perform their partnership tasks. As much as possible, it is important to build opportunities for collaboration into the school day rather than after hours. Of course, the addition of a family/school partnership coordinator to assist the faculty is most welcome.

THE POLITICS OF PARTNERSHIPS

Understanding the political aspect of partnerships is a key to forming and maintaining relationships with the different parties. It may seem strange to link politics with partnerships since family/school partnerships are characterized by trust, caring, and positive regard.

The mention of politics immediately conjures up thoughts of bureaucratic sludge, red tape, waste, corruption, and partisan bickering. While it is true that often the word "politics" is associated with negative outcomes, in this situation I would like us to think about the political process in a generic way.

Back in 1936, Laswell defined politics as: "who gets what, when, and how." This is a good, straightforward definition and fits the political context of a partnership. We are all motivated by self-interests to get what we want. If the term "self-interests" seems a bit harsh, then the word "needs" can be substituted. However, I maintain that the act of influencing others to meet our self-interests is what the political process is about.

While this may sound very manipulative, meeting our self-interests by influencing others is inherently neither a positive nor a negative act. For example, if you have a good relationship with your "significant other," then each of you is meeting some of your self-interests through the relationship. When this occurs, you would say that you have an enduring partnership. And, the partnership will last as long as both of you continue to feel that your self-interests are being met.

With family/school partnerships, the phrase in the definition, "to produce positive educational and social effects on the child, while being mutually beneficial to all other parties involved," relates to the political process. While the child's self-interests are the main focus of the partnership, the other parties also wish to have some of their self-interests or needs satisfied. For the partnership to be effective and long lasting, therefore, the relationship must meet some of the needs of the parents, teachers, and principals as well as the child's.

We may initially be able to get educators and family members excited about entering into a partnership, but it will be hard, if not impossible, to keep them actively involved and committed if they do not see some direct payoff for themselves. To illustrate this point, I often use a popular liquid diet advertisement as a metaphor. The advertisement guarantees that you will lose weight if you, "drink a delicious shake for breakfast and lunch" and "eat a sensible meal at night."

My guess is that many people follow the first direction, but not the second. As a result, the diet program does not work for them because they did not adhere to both requirements. Likewise, in partnership, the self-interests of all stakeholders have to be addressed for the relationship to work. In other words, if the child's needs are met, but not the self-interests of the other parties, the partnership will suffer.

Therefore, knowing and understanding the political process is important when planning, implementing, and maintaining a family/school partnership. It is essential that we identify the self-interests of all the parties: the child, families, and school. We need to ask ourselves: "What are the things, in addition to the concern for the children, that will influence the different parties to be active partners?" Determining what the different stakeholders want and need will help decide what strategies to use to create and build the partnerships.

The self-interests of the families vary greatly. Meeting the self-interests of some families and getting them to be partners is not always complicated, however. Letting them know you care and that you would like to work with them may be enough to get them involved. In these cases, something as simple as a phone call or a personal note may be sufficient to influence their self-interests.

In other instances, incentives such as food, door prizes, child care, and transportation are effective in helping to bring the families to school for conferences, parenting meetings, open houses, and so forth. All of these strategies should send the message, "You and your needs are important to us."

Many hard-to-reach parents feel alienated and disenfranchised from the school and with society as a whole. As a result, strategies need to be implemented to bridge the gaps between the families and the school. Best practices such as neighborhood meetings and home visits must be used to overcome the barriers and meet the families' self-interests.

Some families face severe problems, such as lack of food or clothing, health issues, drug abuse, and so on. These problems will have to be solved before the families affected are able to focus on their children's educational needs. For these parents, the adage, "It is difficult to think about swamp control when you are over your waist in alligators," comes to mind. It is difficult for these families to be thinking about the future of their children when they are trying to survive the day.

The school can use the Coordinating Strategy to help the families to apply for food stamps and other social programs, find a job, and so on.

The need to provide programs to help families in these situations is analogous to the problem that necessitates having a free student breakfast program at school. Besides the humanitarian reason, the educational argument for having the program is that if the kids are hungry, it is hard for them to concentrate on learning. The breakfast program eliminates a barrier.

With the needy families, once some of the pressing concerns are taken care of, the parents can be influenced to focus their attention on the children's social and educational needs. The Coordinating Strategy chapter (Chapter 8) presents examples of programs and activities to get community resources to the families in need.

Unfortunately, if we do not reach out to the underserved families, a typical parent involvement program can actually widen the gap between the "haves and have nots." Many traditional parent involvement programs and activities are oriented toward the middle class, thereby missing the other segments of the school community. Many families feel that they do not fit in with the core group of parents that are controlling the programs. The Self-Renewing Partnership Model presented in chapter 5 is designed to involve all families, but it is especially useful for reaching and empowering the underserved or hard-to-reach parents.

THE BENEFITS OF A FAMILY/SCHOOL PARTNERSHIP

As we develop partnerships, we need to be clear about the positive outcomes for all the stakeholders. The following is a summary of positive outcomes that can be expected from partnerships between the family and school:

Benefits to the School

- better communications between school and home
- improved student behavior
- enhanced social and interpersonal relationships between students
- greater acceptance and understanding of students and families from other cultures
- reduction of in-school violence
- better working conditions for faculty and staff
- improved attitudes and relationships and better communication between teachers and families
- greater family participation in school programs and activities
- schools being more accessible and user-friendly to families
- more family/school activities
- families viewing the school and faculty/staff more favorably
- families having a feeling of ownership, belonging, and inclusion concerning the school

Benefits to the Students

- increased achievement and motivation
- more positive attitude toward school and school work
- higher quality and more appropriate homework
- increased attendance
- decrease in dropouts, suspensions, and discipline referrals
- better relationships with family
- improved feelings about self

Benefits to the Family

- increased empowerment and education
- improved family life and closer relationship with children
- greater school support of families
- better communication between home and school
- increased understanding of school's curriculum, programs, and activities
- increased knowledge about how to help the child
- greater opportunities to engage in learning activities at home
- greater opportunities to work closely with teachers
- more consistent expectations, practices, and messages about homework and home-learning activities
- increased access to schoolwide resources such as family resource centers; homework, telephone, and Internet systems; home visits; classes; and workshops
- greater opportunities to shape important decisions that enhance their child's chance for success in school

Benefits to the Teachers

- improved morale
- more positive teaching experiences
- greater feelings of accomplishment and success
- more support, appreciation, and trust of families' judgment
- fewer discipline problems
- more responsive students
- less stress and frustration
- greater awareness of family perspectives and less stereotyping of students and their families
- higher expectations of students
- closer relationships with students

Benefits to the Administrators

- improved relationships with students and family
- fewer family complaints
- better use of limited resources to address the critical need of linking home and school
- increased communications from family members about the child that is not available in any other way
- greater family support for school bonds and needed school improvements

SUMMARY

Since a family/school partnership is based upon mutual trust, caring, and respect, the school's organizational culture must exhibit these characteristics if it is going to effectively develop and nurture partnerships with the families. If the faculty and staff feel that their efforts are appreciated and are convinced that their suggestions and recommendations will be thoroughly considered, they are more likely to be willing to reach out and empower the parents.

When the partnerships are working, the school will be more responsible to the families and the families more responsible to the school and ultimately, the children will be affected positively by this alliance.

Do family/school partnerships sound a bit like Camelot? Are the outcomes too idealistic? Not really. I have seen the partnerships work and they are effective and energizing. The Self-Renewing Partnership Model presented in chapter 5 is designed to help schools and communities create these collaborative relationships whereby all parties are fully involved in the academic and social development of the children.

However, many barriers have to be overcome to create and maintain effective family/school partnerships. The following chapter describes and discusses the sources of barriers that keep families and the school apart.

Chapter 4

Barriers: Gaps to Overcome

All too often when schools attempt to involve the parents, they get little or no response. The teachers and principals conclude the family members just don't care and that the parents are not interested in being involved. As a result, the schools, which are already overburdened, tend to give up trying to involve the families. It is easy to understand how the educators would reach this conclusion.

However, the results of my research (Lueder, 1989) indicate that the opposite is true. Most families care about the future of their children and are interested in their children's education. But, even if the parents believe they should be involved, what is keeping many of them from being more involved then? Why are there so many parents missing-in-action and hard-to-reach?

Often, there are barriers between the parents and the school that need to be overcome before a family/school partnership can be created. Such barriers can be family-based, school-based, or a combination. One of the functions of the outreach dimension of the Self-Renewing Partnership Model presented in the next chapter is to reduce the gaps between the families and school. The present chapter discusses the sources of the barriers that can keep the families and the schools apart.

FAMILY-BASED BARRIERS

Several family-based barriers can separate the parents from the school. Some sources of these barriers are psychological (e.g., apprehension, fear, alienation) while others are physical (e.g., time, distance, lack of child care).

Lack of skills and knowledge, especially with hard-to-reach parents, can also cause a major barrier. While such things as lower socioeconomic conditions and divorce can be factors in making some parents hard to reach, they are not necessarily causal variables. I believe the following barriers are the major contributors to gaps that may exist between the families and the school.

Psychological Barriers

Many family members don't ask the school for assistance or information because they don't feel connected with the school. These families often are intimidated and perceive the schools as unapproachable and threatening. In fact, it is not unusual for families, especially those living in distressed communities, to mistrust and fear the schools.

Crew and Dyja (2007) argue that some of these families are "supply" parents who feel like outsiders in the very schools that are suppose to be serving them. These reluctant and hesitant parents are among those who have been deemed to be hard to reach.

The psychological gap between the school and the family can be exacerbated if the family members experienced failure in school themselves. Usually, parents' attitudes toward school are rooted in their own educational background. Not only do they distrust the school, they also try to avoid an environment where they had a bad experience.

What makes it even worse is that the parents see their experiences repeated with their children. The family members assume the school will also fail their children if the school failed them. This self-defeating outlook adds to the parents' sense of alienation from the schools and increases the barriers.

Physical Barriers

Many families would like to take a more active role in the education of their children, but their home situation is such that they are struggling to just keep things together. They do not believe they can find more time, resources, or energy to do more. As they deal with their busy schedules, problems, and other pressures, involvement in the education of children gets pushed aside. In fact, for some parents, making sure their children make it to school is a major accomplishment.

Physical barriers, though more common in low-income homes, are not limited to poorer families. Often the lack of time and energy is a problem for middle- and upper-class households as well, especially when the parent or parents are working outside the home.

Lack of Skills and Knowledge

A large number of family members lack the skills and knowledge necessary to be fully involved parents. Many of the hard-to-reach parents would like to be involved, but they don't know what to do. Educating children is a complex and difficult task and often families have not been prepared to assume the different Parent Partner Roles.

The need for more skills and knowledge varies greatly among families. For example, some families may only need information about the nature and function of upcoming conferences and meetings, while others may be seeking classes in conflict resolution or adolescent behavior. Yet, other families may need training on how to help their children with learning activities at home, or want help with issues like nutrition, communication, discipline, drug abuse, and teenage pregnancy.

The hard-to-reach families are often hit with a combination of barriers. For example, parents may feel disconnected with the school and also be inadequately equipped to play the roles necessary to be fully involved in the educational and social development of their children. Some families may be faced with severe problems and not know where or how to get help. For these reasons, it is so important to understand the family needs, cultures, and concerns. With this information, appropriate intervention strategies can be selected and implemented.

NORMATIVE BARRIERS (FAMILY AND SCHOOL)

Some barriers that prevent partnerships from forming between the families and schools, are rooted in long-standing beliefs and perceptions about the roles of parents, teachers, and principals. Some see education as the sole responsibility of the school. They see the role of the families as supporting the school's curriculum, programs, and activities. The traditional approach to parent involvement is based on this perception.

Seeley (1985, 1989) contends that this belief has caused a delivery system mentality wherein the schools believe, inaccurately, that they should be the only providers of educational services. The result is a sort of isolationism from the families. In turn, the families' reaction to the delivery model is to adopt a delegation model, where they feel they do not have to, and are not expected to, be involved with school. These attitudes are clearly self-defeating and lead to barriers.

When education is seen as delegated to one party, as opposed to being a collaborative process, gaps between the families and the schools will develop.

One result of this isolationalism is that when problems occur, the parents tend to blame the teachers whereas the teachers are apt to blame the parents. This creates a no-win situation for the families and the school, but especially for the children.

Lightfoot (1978) suggests the history of home-school relationships indicates that families and schools are inclined to be adversaries because of the nature of the relationship: Parents focus on their own child's needs, while the school has to be concerned with the needs of all the children in the school. Consequently, there is a natural pull between what the parents feel the school should be doing for their child and what the school feels it can do for all the children. Lightfoot argues that schools avoid dealing with this potential conflict by adopting brief, ritualized encounters when they do have to involve the parents.

Such activities as open houses and PTA meetings are cited as contrived events that are advertised as opportunities for a partnership, but are actually organized in such a way that little or no authentic interaction can occur. These traditional events can be refined to reflect the partnership philosophy, however. These changes are discussed in the Communicating Strategy chapter (chapter 7).

While I agree that "isolationalism" does exist in many settings and that certain norms are setting the families and schools apart, I do not believe these conditions are inherent in the relationships. The relationship between the school and the families does not have to be adversarial. However, it would be naïve to believe that conflict will not occur. Issues involving such things as children with special needs, student assignments, budget cuts, and overcrowding are fraught with differing beliefs, perceptions, and interests.

However, even with these issues, most families and schools want to work together, but they may need help in doing it. I have worked with schools to help form partnerships based on trust, respect, and mutual regard. Such partnerships have been very effective. However, any negative attitudes and beliefs have to be dealt with first.

If true partnerships between the families and school are to occur, the different parties need to perceive that education is everyone's responsibility. For this to happen, the principal and teachers must actively pursue family participation. Both the families and the school must agree that they have a common goal, which is to educate the children.

Over 30 years ago, Comer (1980) argued, "Rather than considering work with parents an extra burden, schools should think of it as an opportunity to educate students and parents at the same time. A school has an opportunity to help children learn in the classroom when it helps parents develop skills" (p.144).

While I agree with Comer, getting the faculty and staff to reach out to families is sometimes difficult. As a result, it is often necessary to work with the faculty and staff to help them understand and accept the concept that having the families as partners will not only help the children, but also will help them.

If data suggest that some parents are uncomfortable with the school, the faculty and staff need to look at themselves and determine how accurate the families' perceptions are. Specifically, they should determine if there are things the school is doing, or not doing, that are keeping the parents and school apart.

It is important to keep in mind that even if you find that the parents' perceptions are inaccurate—that in fact, the teachers and principals do want the parents in the school—the parents' perceptions are still real to them. As a result, the families' perceptions need to be changed to bring about participation.

There is another normative barrier that is more subtle. As indicated in the previous chapter, many parent involvement programs are based on a middle-class value system, and as a result, may create barriers in and of themselves.

Rich (1987) believes that all parents want the best for their children, but that some do not feel comfortable participating in the traditional school activities. Henderson (1986) points out the disparities between values, attitudes, expectations, and behaviors of poor minority families and the middle-class values, attitudes, expectations, and behaviors that are enshrined in most schools. For some families that feel that they do not fit into the system, some parent involvement program can actually increase the gaps.

The school can implement programs to reduce the gaps between social classes, however. By bringing the families, teachers, and principals together, the sense of estrangement is reduced and the school environment becomes far less threatening and more conducive to learning for both students and parents.

SUMMARY

The various barriers that are preventing family involvement cause problems not only for the children, but for the school as well. The children are the messengers of our future and we cannot afford to lose them. It is increasingly apparent that the school must assume the responsibility of helping many of the families to create appropriate home environments and to enhance the skills and knowledge needed to play the different parenting roles. Otherwise, we have little chance of being able to support and educate all children. The Self-Renewing Partnership Model presented in the next chapter has been developed to help the schools meet the challenge of overcoming barriers and involving all families, especially the hard-to-reach.

Chapter 5

The Self-Renewing Partnership Model: Energy-Out and Energy-In

The Self-Renewing Partnership Model is a powerful conceptual framework for creating partnerships between the families and school, especially with hard-to-reach parents. The model differs radically from the traditional parent involvement approach, described in chapter 1. Whereas, the primary goal of most traditional programs is to increase family support for the school's curriculum and program, the goals of the Self-Renewing Partnership Model are more focused and comprehensive.

That is, the purpose of this model is to fully involve all of the families in their children's education both in the home and at school. Figure 5.1 is a diagram of the Self-Renewing Partnership Model.

The model has two dimensions that interact and build on each other. These dimensions are labeled "energy-out" and "energy-in" to indicate the directions that the resources flow. The energy-in dimension encompasses the eight Parent Partner Roles, described in chapter 2.

It is called "energy-in" because as the families play their parenting roles, their resources (time, money, expertise, etc.) are directed *in* at the children and *in* at the school. This dimension is an expansion of the traditional "families supporting the school" approach. However, more resources from the fully-involved parents are flowing to the school, and much of the energy is concentrated on the child.

The energy-out dimension has four Partnership Intervention strategies. The schools use these strategies to reach *out* and work with the families. It is the energy-out dimension that makes the Self-Renewing Partnership Model unique and effective. With its function to reach out and help get the parents involved, it is the energy-out dimension that jumpstarts the partnership process. It cannot be emphasized enough that reaching out to the parents is the key to connecting with and involving the missing families.

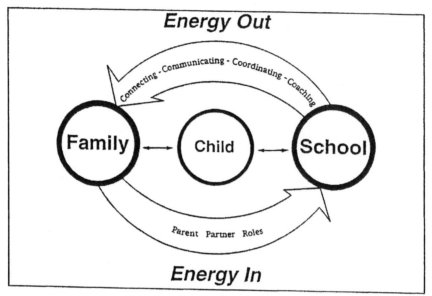

Figure 5.1

A SHIFT IN PARADIGMS

Reaching out to the families of course is not the norm in most schools and communities today. As indicated earlier, the outward flow energy is a radical change from the traditional approach to parent involvement. Consequently, for the energy-out dimension to work, the involvement of the families must be viewed in a different way.

The term "paradigm shift" has been used recently to describe major changes in the way people perceive an issue or condition. A paradigm is your view of the world based on your personal frame of reference. Paradigms provide a way to organize a large amount of data in order to identify relationships and give meaning through context.

According to Covey (1992), a paradigm is "your scheme for understanding and explaining certain aspects of reality." He contends that if we want to make major changes, we need to shift our paradigm and perceive the issue in a totally new way.

To accept that reaching out to families is a necessary step to create partnerships, especially with hard-to-reach parents, the schools and families must make a shift in the way they think about themselves and their mission. It involves an attitude shift. Teachers, counselors, and principals must believe that they need to be involved with such activities as home visits, neighborhood town meetings, parenting classes, family resource centers, and support groups.

This means that we have to embrace a new paradigm and give up our present one. We have to be convinced that the old model is not working before we are willing to accept a new one. It is difficult to convince people to give up their current way of thinking, especially if it requires they use scarce resources (time, money, etc.) to treat the sources and not the symptoms.

For example, in most schools and communities, we know that we can do better; yet, we are not completely dissatisfied with what is happening now. Therefore, we are reluctant to reject the present model and go through the process of introducing and accepting a new one. Developing new roles and relationships can be very frightening, so we tend to hold tight and not change.

Sometimes it is easier to make educational changes in distressed schools because it is clear that the old model isn't working. In these situations, the teachers, principals, and families are more apt to be willing and eager to find a different way to help the children and themselves.

A *"Light Bulb" Experience*

An encounter I had with a principal in California helped clarify the "energy-out" dimension and the need for a paradigm shift. A school district asked me to provide staff development training for their Chapter I Family/School Coordinators. Since I was in the district already, the superintendent suggested that I meet with his principals and share my parent involvement ideas and research. I agreed, and we gathered in a large lecture room. Right after I was introduced, a principal in the back of the room stood and said, "What could you possibly tell me about parent involvement that I don't already know? I have a terrific parent involvement program at my school."

I responded, "I'm not sure I can tell you anything that you do not already know. Would you share with me what you are doing at your school?"

He told how he was able to get many of his parents to come to school and do volunteer work. They helped supervise students in the classrooms and cafeteria, copy materials, and answer the office telephone.

As he described his program, a "light went on." His concept of parent involvement was very different from mine. He thought of parent involvement only as family members coming to school to help, whereas, I perceived parent involvement as being much more than that. For me, parent involvement means the family members are actively engaged in the education of their children at home and at school.

It became clear that to accept the energy-out dimension, he would have to abandon his traditional parent involvement approach and embrace the concept of family/school partnerships. After introducing the notion of partnerships and having further discussions with him after the meeting, I sensed that he was interested in trying to help his school to make the shift.

PARTNERSHIP INTERVENTION STRATEGIES: THE BIG C'S

As stated earlier, the Self-Renewing Partnership Model differs radically from other parent involvement models because of its energy-out dimension. The dimension is composed of a series of progressive Partnership Intervention strategies. The four strategies are: connecting, communicating, coordinating, and coaching. The school uses the various strategies to overcome barriers between the school and the families, build collaborative relationships, coordinate resources, and help the parents to play their Parent Partner Roles.

Specifically, the strategies are used to make connections, develop two-way communication flows, and coordinate needed services and resources. Once collaborative relationships are established with the families, the Coaching Strategy is used to involve and empower the family members by enhancing their parenting skills and knowledge. The following is a summary of the functions of the Partnership Intervention Strategies:

The Connecting Strategy is designed to:

- prepare the school to reach out and connect with the families
- create an inviting and helpful school environment where the family members and faculty/staff can comfortably interact with each other
- overcome any psychological or physical barriers that might be preventing the families from working with the school
- begin to build collaborative relationships with the families
- initiate two-way communication flows between the families and the school

The Communicating Strategy is designed to:

- establish two-way communication flows between the families and the school
- continue to build collaborative relationships with the families
- begin to increase family for the school's programs and activities

The Coordinating Strategy is designed to:

- increase family awareness of availability of school and community services and resources
- ensure that school and community services and resources are accessible to all families in need
- facilitate the creation of new services and resources
- organize family and community resources to help support the school's curriculum and programs

The Coaching Strategy is designed to:

- enhance parents' ability and capacity to effectively play the parent partner roles
- enhance the parents' general sense of well-being, knowledge, and skill level

The functions listed under each of the strategies are also the objectives of the family/school partnership program.

THE PROGRESSIVE NATURE OF THE PARTNERSHIP INTERVENTION STRATEGIES

Like the Parent Partner Roles, the Partnership Intervention Strategies are progressive. That is, the strategies build upon each other. For example, you need to be connected with the families before you can communicate, and you have to be communicating before services and resources can be coordinated. Before parents can be coached, barriers need to be overcome and collaborative relationships need to be established between the families and the school.

Therefore, when forming partnerships with the families, it is necessary to ascertain the characteristics of the targeted family groups and to determine the source and magnitude of any barriers that may exist. After this, the appropriate strategies are selected and best practices are implemented.

In the following chapters, each Partnership Intervention Strategy is described and discussed, including an array of best practices that the school can use to implement the strategies.

THE "SELF-RENEWING" PHENOMENON

The interactions between the energy-out and energy-in dimensions result in a self-renewing system. When the energy-out dimension (The Partnership Intervention Strategies) impacts on the families, the energy-in dimension (Parent Partner Roles) becomes more active and effective.

Because of the school's intervention, the parents are more involved with the children's education in the home, and with the school, through parent education workshops and classes, parent/teacher conferences, open houses, volunteer programs, and curriculum committees.

The interaction between the energy-out and energy-in dimension is a synergistic relationship. This means that by interacting the two dimensions generate more energy than originally existed; the whole is greater than the sum of its parts. As the school reaches out and empowers the families, the families become more energized and direct more of their resources toward the children and the school.

And, as the family's energy-in dimension is enhanced, it strengthens the collaborative relationship with the school and creates more power for the school's energy-out dimension. This power increase in the energy-out dimension results in more energy going out and impacting the families.

Thus, the term "self-renewing" is used to indicate the synergistic relationship, or integrated circuit between the two components. When a family/school partnership is working effectively, it perpetuates itself. All parties are empowered by the collaborative relationships are continually "renewed."

While all parties in the partnership benefit from the "energy loop," we must keep in mind that the ultimate beneficiaries of the partnerships are the children. The partnerships are not ends in themselves, but a means to impact the educational and social development of the children.

SUMMARY

It is my firm belief that if all children are going to receive the kind of help and support they need, we must reach out to assist families to be fully functioning parent partners. This is why I am advocating that schools use some of their resources to create family/school partnerships. As the families learn to play their Parent Partner Roles, the children will receive the needed support at home and the schools will receive more support from the families.

The families have to be connected with the school; two-way communication flows must exist between the school and the families; and parents must be empowered to play their Parent Partner Roles, both at home and at school. The Partnership Intervention Strategies described in the following chapters have been designed to help the schools and communities to reach out and create partnerships.

Chapter 6

Connecting Strategy: Bridging the Gaps

Table 6.1

Connecting	Communicating	Coordinating	Coaching

Unfortunately, it is common for the schools to invite the families to participate in meetings, conferences, and activities and then only have a few family members show up. When this happens, it is easy to understand why teachers and administrators get the impression that the families are not interested in being involved.

In reality, however, the reason the families are avoiding the school is not that they do not care—instead, many parents do not feel connected with the school. This is usually because of psychological or physical barriers blocking the way. As discussed in chapter 4, there are many different sources for the barriers.

Many families do not get involved because they are anxious, apprehensive, and even fearful about dealing with teachers and principals. In some cases, family members feel so out of place they are disenfranchised from the school and society as a whole. For other families, logistical barriers such as conflicting work schedules, lack of child care, and no transportation prevent them from getting involved.

On the other hand, schools may also be creating barriers. School-based barriers can result from impersonal or demeaning behavior by the faculty and staff, unfortunate school policies, or faculty and staff not knowing how to work with parents.

I cannot emphasize enough that parent involvement programs are often ineffective because they are implemented without large segments of the family populations being connected. As a result, these hard-to-reach parents do not respond to the school's messages and are not impacted by the programs. By reaching out and letting the families know that schools care and are willing to help, and would like to work with them, the chances of creating a partnership with the underserved families improve dramatically.

As stated in the previous chapter, the Partnership Intervention Strategies are progressive and hierarchical, with the Connecting Strategy being the most basic intervention. The connections between the school and the families provide the foundation for the other three Partnership Intervention Strategies. Partnerships are created by making connections, establishing two-way communication flows, coordinating resources and services, and coaching the families.

Connecting with the parents is the first step in creating a family/school partnership. Therefore, the Connecting Strategy is designed to:

- prepare the school to reach out and connect with the families
- create an inviting and helpful environment where the families and faculty/staff can comfortably interact with each other
- overcome any psychological or physical barriers that might be preventing the families and the school from working together
- begin to build collaborative relationships with the families
- initiate two-way communication flows between the families and school

CONNECTING BEST PRACTICES

The following sections present best practices that the school can use to implement the Connecting Strategy. To help the readers locate and select appropriate best practices, the programs, activities, and events are grouped around the following categories:

- creating user-friendly schools
- group connecting
- one-on-one connecting
- preparing the faculty and staff to reach out

The best practices in the first three categories are intended to overcome family-based barriers, whereas the practices in the last category are directed at school-based barriers. Since the process of making connections with the families is developmental and incremental, in some cases, several best practices may be needed over a period of time. Also, the degree of disconnection that parents feel varies from family to family. Consequently, some best practices are directed at the disconnected family populations while others are more general in nature and intend to reach the families that are on the verge of being connected.

Making connections with the hard-to-reach families usually requires a sustained comprehensive effort. It is important to be patient and stay the course when attempting to build collaborative relationships with distressed families.

The intent and purpose of the intervention must be clear when choosing the best practices. A particular best practice can serve several purposes, so the outcomes depend upon what is emphasized as the practice is being used. For example, a telephone call is an effective connecting best practice when the focus is to overcome barriers and initiate a relationship. However, if a family is already connected, the primary purpose of the call is to build a relationship and convey useful information. The formation of a relationship is a dynamic process and the facilitator must decide what to emphasize as the relationship unfolds.

Creating User-Friendly Schools

Making the school environment welcoming, inviting, and helpful as possible is an important bridge to connect the faculty and staff with the families. A school is a complex bureaucracy and can easily be perceived as impersonal and threatening. The explicit and implicit message to the families should be: "You are welcome, you are important to us, and we want to work with you to educate your children."

Welcome signs. At many schools, the first thing families read when they come to school is the statement: "All visitors *must* report to the office." This stern message can be a real turn off.

Some might argue that the negative signs are necessary for security reasons. Certainly, security is important, but I doubt if negative signs are very effective.

When discussing this issue with groups, I facetiously tell them that when I travel, I stop by schools to sell drugs and abuse teachers. When I arrived at the school, I immediately go to the office and sign in. I make sure I let the principal or secretary know where I will be loitering in school so I don't miss anyone.

Of course, the point is that the individuals for whom the negative signs are intended, like drug dealers and abusers, will not heed the notice.

Since the parents and community members are the ones who usually see and read the signs, why not display a more positive message such as:

"Welcome, parents and other visitors. To better serve you and the students, please come by the office so we can assist you."

Most visitors understand the need for security and have no problem being asked to check in at the office. The positive signs will give parents and visitors better feelings, perceptions, and expectations about the school and their visit.

A Family Doorbell

At a middle school located in a distressed community with a high-crime rate, the doors of the school were locked during and after the school day. Soon after the family/school coordinator began working at the school, she noticed that when the parents came to the school they had to pound on the door to get in. Usually, it took a long time before anyone responded, and sometimes, the family members just gave up and left.

Since it was felt necessary that the doors stay locked, the coordinator worked with the school's principal to install a doorbell that rang in the office. Different staff members are now responsible for answering the door in a friendly and helpful manner. Installing the bell removed, one of the physical barriers keeping the family from being part of the school.

Parent parking spaces. Providing reserved parking spaces for parents is not only a convenience, but also a strong symbolic gesture that says to the family members, "You are important and we value you." Think of the message you are sending when on a rainy day parents find a space waiting for them, so they can park near the door and not get wet.

Label the spaces, "Parents/Visitors," if you have limited space and you need to allocate parking for other visitors. You can receive many positive points for this parking practice.

Office manners. Observe how secretaries and other staff members greet family members on the phone or in person. Think about the kind of impression they are making, and whether they are being helpful.

Emphasize the importance of being responsive and caring. Point out they are usually the first person whom visitors come in contact with. I have found I learn a lot about a school's culture from the way I am greeted when arriving at the office.

Also, remind the teachers and staff how they greet and interact with parents and visitors in the hallways and other school areas is equally important. Visitors' perceptions of the school's curriculum, programs, and faculty are often based on the first interaction they have with someone at the school.

Coffee and tea connections. Have coffee, tea, juice, or soft drinks available when parents and visitors arrive at school for a meeting or conference. Serve the beverage in cups or glasses bearing the school's collective vision, mission statement, or logo. Not only is this a symbolic gesture about the importance of the visit, but also it is an opportunity to promote the school's commitment to education and the families.

School maps. It is important to have a school map at the school's entrances showing how to get to the office. How many times have you arrived at a school and wandered around trying to locate the office? Colorful signs, in different languages if needed, can be used to direct visitors to where they need to go.

Teacher-made posters. Henderson, et al. (2007) report the teachers at the Corpus Christi middle schools made posters that described themselves and placed them outside the classrooms. The posters described such things as their backgrounds, interests, hobbies, and their favorite books. The posters had pictures of the teachers at different ages and them doing fun things.

Those of us who are teachers, know the reaction of the students when they see you at the grocery store, "Wow: you actually shop for food?" This best practice helped the students and parents see the teachers as real people. It's great.

School directory. Publish a school directory that includes pictures of the teachers and staff. This can be handed out to visitors or at meetings. The directory can also be posted on the school's website.

Bulletin board. Pictures of the teachers and staff can be placed on a bulletin board in the school's lobby. Information about room numbers can be posted as well.

Partnership policy. Display the school's family/school partnership policy in the lobby and around the school. Print copies of the policy and have it available for families members. The policy is an official announcement of the school's commitment to parent involvement. If you have no policy, bring school faculty and staff, and family members together to develop one.

Attempt to reach a consensus about the importance of reaching out and involving all families. Present the proposed family/school partnership policy to the school board, school improvement council, school management and planning team, PTA, and so on, for their approval.

Family of the month. A picture of the "Family/Families of the Month" can be displayed as part of the school's lobby program. Faculty and staff can nominate families based on partnership activities the parents have been involved in with the child or the school.

One caution, while this is a nice way of acknowledging involvement by a family member, there can be a downside if the practice becomes too competitive or inclusive. Recognizing several families at a time and nominating parents from all segments of the population can prevent elitism and a feeling that only middle-class values are emphasized.

Partnership photo albums. Place photograph albums in the lobby, main office, and parent room for families and visitors to browse through. Such albums consist of pictures of partnership events and activities such as volunteering, celebrations, awards, social events, and volunteering. Family members and children love to see pictures of themselves. When possible, send copies of pictures to the families and the local newspapers.

Welcome wagon. To make the families more comfortable with the school, a committee of faculty, parents, and community volunteers can form a welcome wagon support program. The welcome wagon members act as hosts/hostesses during registration times and the first days of school. The welcome wagon committee also schedules connecting events at different times of the year to create a positive school environment. This is also a good service for families and students who are transitioning from elementary to middle schools.

New family tours. Provide a tour of the school for new students and their families. Having a student from the new student's grade level helping with the tour can make the connection with the school.

Best buddies. A student version of the welcome wagon group is a program called "Best Buddies." Students volunteer to act as school ambassadors at programs and activities, greeting families and visitors and providing directions and tours. The student volunteers directed the family members to appropriate places and answered questions. At one school, the best buddies help family members when they came to school to register their children. Also, the best buddies program is very useful for transitioning events when students and families are moving from elementary to middle school or from middle to high school.

Parent/family centers. Establish centers or rooms in the school where family members can come for information, support, and training. Some schools use the term "parent center," others use "family center." The latter term acknowledges the whole family's involvement and indirectly welcomes grandparents, aunts, uncles, siblings, and other relatives. No matter which term is used, the families should feel that the facilities are available for everyone.

The centers provide an environment that helps make connections and form a community. In some distressed situations, the family center serves as a community center or safe haven.

In a well-equipped center, books, audiotapes, videotapes, games, puzzles, telephones, computers, copying machines, software, and other materials are available for the family's use. Some schools even provide kitchens, laundry rooms, and sewing machines. Schools can approach businesses, industry and service groups for donations to buy equipment, supplies, and software. A section describing the use of the centers to coordinate services and resources for needy families is presented in chapter 8.

Underwear Link

Matt Benningfield, former principal of the Dann C. Byck Elementary School in Kentucky, used an effective best practice for many years to connect with

new mothers in the neighborhood. When a baby was born, he sent a congratu-
lation card attached to an infant-sized undershirt. The bottom of the shirt was
pinned shut and was filled with brochures and other information about the
school and community services, as well as materials about parenting, home
learning, and other topics. The undershirt provided an innovative link with the
school from birth and invited the parent to be a partner from the start.

Self-help workshops and classes. A variety of parent education programs
and activities can be offered to make connections and meet a variety of family needs. For example, high school diploma equivalency, literacy, English
language, and adolescent psychology classes are popular. The events do not
need to be limited to school-oriented topics, but can focus on such concerns
as daycare, recreation, personal health, drug abuse, crime, and violence.

Styling and Profiling

At an elementary school in Nashville, the parents were invited to volun-
teer to be "clients" for a cosmetology class at a nearby comprehensive high
school. The students needed individuals to practice on for haircuts, styling,
permanents, hair coloring, and manicures. The parents could fill this need.
The parents loved to have their hair and nails done, and were eager to volun-
teer. The activity was directed at the self-interests of both the parents and the
cosmetology students. As a result, the best practice made connections with the
families and the students got their clients.

A large portion of the Coaching Strategy chapter (chapter 9) is devoted to
parent education best practices designed to enhance the families' capacity to
effectively play their Parent Partner Roles. Many of these best practices can
also help with connecting.

Coupon exchange center. A place in the school can be set up for parents,
faculty, and staff to exchange coupons for food, services, and other products.
The coupon center can be located in the main office, guidance office, or parent center. Usually, the teachers' lounge is not a good spot if you want the
families to use the coupon exchange center as a gathering place.

Participants place unwanted coupons in a box and can look through the
supply to see if there are coupons they can use. Parent volunteers can sort
through the coupons, categorize them (e.g., food, drinks, cleaning supplies,
paper good, etc.), and place them in files or separate boxes.

Field trips. Invite parents to go along with their children on field trips to
libraries, fire houses, television and radio stations, newspaper offices, airports,
hospitals, court houses, police stations, parks, museums, factories, and so on. I
have found that family members have never visited many of these places. They
will be anxious to go, and it will be a good learning experience for everyone.

Connecting With Feeder Schools

As students transition from one school to another, it is important for the families to be oriented to the new school. In some cases, parents do not even know where the new school is located. In one metropolitan school district, kindergarten students go to school in their neighborhoods, but busing begins with the first grade. At one inner-city school, the parents were putting their kids on a bus and had no idea where the children were going. The school was located about eight miles away and the families had never visited the school. Most families did not have transportation and they did not know how to get to the school if they did have a means to get there.

To solve the problem, orientation meetings were scheduled at the "feeder" school and the families were transported to the new school. Family members toured the building, met with teachers, guidance counselors, and principals, and had an opportunity to ask questions and share their concerns.

School vegetable garden. A school vegetable garden is a way to build support, and provide lessons in cooperation, giving, health, and nutrition. Family members, students, teachers, principals, and other staff members work together to plan, plant, cultivate, and harvest the garden.

Usually, there is a plot of land on the school grounds or nearby in the neighborhood that can be made available for a garden. In one school neighborhood, the land under some electric power lines was used.

Everyone shares the crop. Sometimes the garden is so large that there are enough vegetables to give to senior citizens living at home and to nursing homes. Not only are the recipients pleased and grateful, but also sharing the harvest is a demonstration of the collaborative spirit.

School flower garden. A variation, or addition, to the school vegetable garden is a flower garden. Not only do the participants get fresh cut flowers for their use at home, but also flowers are given to "shut-ins" and senior citizens, hospitals, and retirement and nursing homes. Local garden clubs or horticulture classes can be asked to help with planning the garden.

Opening school facilities to families. Adopt a community school philosophy, where the school is believed to be for everyone's use. Arrange for the school facilities to be available to families for recreation, classes, support groups, and other meetings.

Libraries, media centers, gymnasiums, and pools are open to family members after school and during weekends. Not only will the family members feel connected by using the facilities, but also will take ownership for the school. If school funds are not available for supervision and other costs, businesses and service clubs can be asked for their support by volunteering time to work with the family members and to raise funds.

Group Connecting

Logistics

Being flexible in the location and timing of group events can overcome some of the physical barriers. Providing transportation and child care is also helpful. The following are a few logistical suggestions:

- The events can be held at school or in the community at churches, community centers, hospital cafeterias, and so forth. The location of the social activity should depend upon where the families live, how comfortable they are with the school, the availability of facilities, and so on. Be flexible and plan accordingly.
- Provide name tags so it is easier for the family members and the faculty and staff to meet each other. Sometimes, when making up name tags for the families, or asking the family members to, include the child's name or have the family members list their names as Cindy's mom or Danny's dad, or whatever is appropriate.
- Use a sign-in sheet to get the parents' names, addresses, and telephone numbers. Let them know, if they agree, that the information will be distributed to all the families so they contact each other if they wish. The school uses these data for follow-up communication.
- Give inexpensive door prizes. The prizes can be a variety of new and old items, tickets, food, and so on. Small educational games or toys make excellent prizes. Local businesses are often willing to donate items for prizes. Also, teachers and community volunteers probably have potential prizes (white elephants) stored in their closets, dressers, and so forth, just waiting to be donated.

Social Events

Social events are an excellent way to make connections and build relationships with the families. The events are opportunities for the faculty and staff to bridge the gap. Fun and relaxation should be the focus, with little or no business conducted. Hopefully, the next time a family member sees a teacher or principal he can reminisce about the fun he had.

Breaking Bread

Having a meal together has traditionally been a wonderful means of connecting in most societies. There are an almost unlimited number of ways that food can be used to bring the school and families together. In most cases, the school and community can host these events at little or no cost to the families as businesses and service clubs are usually willing to help with the cost of such events.

Once families are connected and involved, the school and family members can plan the events together and host such things as Thanksgiving day luncheons and Christmas brunches as part of their partnership activities. Examples of social events that are food oriented include:

- Spaghetti dinners—Spaghetti dinners are quite inexpensive to prepare and serve and are also an easy meal for the cafeteria staff to fix.
- Pizza parties—Most families like pizza. Pizzas can be ordered or prepared at school.
- Potluck or pass-the-dish suppers—Families come to the event with a dish to pass (e.g., casseroles, sliced meats, vegetables, salads, etc.). The entrees are set out on large tables to make a buffet. The school supplies drinks, dishes, silverware, and so forth. Usually, the families bring one of their favorite dishes and the results are fantastic.
- Ethnic dinners—These are similar to potluck suppers, but in this case families bring foods native to their cultures to share with others. If facilities are available, family members can even prepare the food on site. With so much diversity in the schools, the event is a wonderful bonding experience for the children and other families.
- Learning community breakfasts—The school hosts a breakfast on a teacher workday for families, faculty, and staff. This early morning get-together is a good way to start the day and make connections.
- Ice cream socials—Almost everyone loves ice cream and these events have been around for a long time. Besides having a selection of flavors, an area for making your own sundae is provided with nuts, chocolate syrup, whipped cream, and so on. Having the teachers and principal serve the ice cream is a nice touch.
- Dessert night—At this event, families, faculty, and staff bring dessert dishes to share. The school supplies coffee, tea, soft drinks, juice, and so on. Again, families from different cultures can bring their favorite dishes.
- Cookie swap party—Similar to the dessert night event, homemade cookies and cakes are brought to the party to be shared with other family members, teachers, principals, and staff. This offers the families an opportunity to show off their favorite cookie. Milk, coffee, and tea are provided by the school.

Family picnics. A great way to build partnerships is for the school to host a family picnic. This can be a back-to-school event where the families, faculty, and staff come together for an evening of informal fun. The picnic provides an opportunity for the families and children to interact with the teachers, and sometimes their families, outside the classroom setting.

Usually, no formal school business is conducted, but tables can be set up where families can pick up information on parenting and social issues, family handbooks, the school curriculum, extracurricular programs, and home-learning activities. Special attention should be made to accommodate all of the various culture represented at the school.

How much the school can provide in food and supplies will depend on the intent, situation, and funding. Generally, the purpose of the picnic is to bring people together as a bonding experience and most families are connected to some degree. Sometimes, the school supplies the drinks and paper goods, while the families bring their own food.

If the event is being staged primarily to connect with hard-to-reach families, the picnic should be free, or very inexpensive. Transportation and child care are also provided. The picnic is a symbolic gesture to the families that they are important, and that you would like them to be partners with the school. Businesses, service clubs, and industries are usually willing to help with the cost.

Playing Together

The school can host a variety of events and activities to bring families and faculty and staff together to have a good time. Parents and children observe the faculty and staff in different roles and see them as real people. By having fun together, the families and teachers are more comfortable with each other. The following are some suggestions for playing together activities:

- Movie night—Videos appropriate for the whole family are shown in the school's auditorium or cafeteria. Films are rented that are fun and have a positive message. Families are encouraged to discuss the meaning of the movies with their children at home. Popcorn and soft drinks are provided.
- Sock-hops—Families, faculty, and staff come together for an old-fashioned sock hop in the school's gymnasium or cafeteria. Music from the 1950s is played with a teacher, family member, or community volunteer acting as a DJ. Everyone is encouraged to dress according to the times (e.g., poodle skirts, peg pants, etc.). Light refreshments are served.
- Bingo parties—Bingo parties are held in the school's cafeteria. Faculty and staff usually have small treasures tucked away in closets that can be used as prizes. Local businesses and store owners can also be approached to donate prizes.
- Yard sale/flea market—Families, faculty, and staff are invited to bring in items that they would like to donate for a school yard sale or flea market.

As with the bingo parties, industries, businesses, and stores are usually also willing to make donations. Entertainment can be provided by the school's band and chorus, groups of students, and community groups. The school makes a little money for future partnership activities while everyone has a good time.

- Spring fling or fall festival—The PTA, School Improvement Council, or other groups organize a school festival or fair for the families and community. Games and activities are arranged for the children and adults, and student art exhibits, band concerts, dance demonstrations, and chorus presentations can also be part of the event. Food and refreshments are available. Sometimes, the fair can be combined with a chicken barbeque or spaghetti dinner.
- Community feast and auction—Tickets are sold in the community for the feast. In addition to the food, a live and silent auction is held. Items to be auctioned are donated by businesses and individuals. One community holds this event as part of the July 4 weekend celebration.
- An angel happening—This is a traditional fund-raising project at an inner-city elementary school's family/school Christmas bazaar. A local craft maker makes ceramic Christmas tree angels especially for the annual event. Each year, the angel is a little different. Families, students, and teachers take advance orders for the angels.

    Learning community members look forward to purchasing the annual edition of the Christmas angel each year. Be aware of the religious make-up of the school community when thinking about using this best practice. You can modify it to fit the situation.
- Faculty/student basketball game—Scheduling a basketball game between the faculty and the students is a good way to connect with the families. Families like to see their kids perform and it is a good time for all.
- Some other events—Once the school and families start to organize events for the learning community, they can also schedule such things as hay and sleigh rides, fishing and hiking trips, and so on.

A Halloween Carnival

A Halloween carnival held each year at an elementary school in Nashville demonstrates the developmental and progressive nature of the Partnership Intervention Strategies. The school is located in a community where previously there was little or no family involvement. The families did not feel connected with the school. Most of the family members had not done well in school themselves and were hesitant to be involved.

During the first year that the school had the carnival, the teachers organized games and contests for the students. The activities were noncompetitive and the students were not pitted against each other. All the students who participated were winners. The families were invited to attend and some of the family members came and watched.

The second year, the family members were asked if they would like to help with the games and activities. Several family members volunteered to assist the teachers. The family members were instructed about the noncompetitive nature of the games and contests and how everyone would be rewarded for doing their best. The parents were connected and began to communicate with the teachers.

By the third year, more and more families were involved with the Halloween carnival and by the fourth year, the families organized and conducted the carnival themselves. As the families became more and more involved, the teachers were able to coach them about responsibility, planning, cooperation, and decision-making. As a result, the carnival became a win-win partnership experience for the students, families, and teachers.

Neighborhood Meetings

Bringing families together with neighborhood events can be an excellent connecting strategy. The following are some examples of neighborhood best practices:

- Family neighborhood forums—Family forums or town meetings are held in the neighborhood to discuss partnership activities and other family and school issues. The location of a meeting is dependent upon how disconnected the families are. If the families are unsure about the schools, it is best to select a neutral or a home location where the families usually gather in their neighborhood. For example, a community center or church may be a better place than a nearby school or housing office if the families don't feel comfortable with schools or the housing authority. This best practice can be used to build the connections or as a means of communication. The families have to feel somewhat connected for this to work.
- Education Sunday parent pledge programs—Presentations are made at churches seeking community support and family involvement. After the presentations, the family members are asked to pledge in writing to encourage learning and success for the children. Of course, this strategy can be adapted to any religion.
- Neighborhood parent/teacher conferences—At times, regular parent-teacher conferences are held in the neighborhoods. This is especially important if the neighborhoods are not near the school as is often the case when busing is involved. Depending upon the type and size of the meeting, if can be held at community centers, housing office conference area, churches, synagogues or other places of worships, youth centers, hospitals, factories,

union halls, Laundromats, and even a nearby school. A special section on conducing parent-teacher conferences is included in the Communicating Strategy chapter (chapter 7).

Fast-Food Connections

A school decided the best place to hold a connecting meeting was at a location where the families hung out a lot. It was determined that a majority of the families frequented a certain fast-food restaurant in the neighborhood. The school made arrangements with the restaurant to host a meeting. Parents and children attending the meeting ate for free, as the restaurant and the school split the cost. To help foster the connections, the principal and teachers put on restaurant uniforms and served the families. The meeting was a huge success.

One-on-One Connecting

For some family populations, more intensive one-on-one best practices are necessary to make connections. Three best practices are particularly effective when attempting to make connections with hard-to-reach families: personal letters, telephone calls, and home visits.

While the activities are similar in intent, they differ in the level of intensity and personal contact. The letter is the least intensive and the home visit is the most. A personal letter may work with families that do not feel alienated, but for the parents who are feeling very out of place, a face-to-face visit is probably the most effective approach.

When working with the disconnected families, always keep in mind that your primary focus is to overcome the barriers and to initiate a collaborative relationship. When making connections, remember to build on the family's strong points. All families have strengths and a sense of pride even though they may be living in poverty or be poorly educated.

The following section presents guidelines for composing letters, making telephone calls, and conducting home visits. The guidelines apply whether you are reaching out to the families, by mail, over the phone, or in person. E-mails have become a popular means of communication, however, they are somewhat impersonal and many hard-to-reach families do not have access to computers.

Guidelines or Letters, Telephone Calls, and Home Visits

The Initial Connecting Attempt

- Begin the letter or conversation by telling a little about yourself.
- Be prepared to say something positive about the child.

- Emphasize how much you want to work with the student and the family.
- Ask about the child's special interests, pets, hobbies, sports, and other outside school activities.
- Explore if the child has any special needs that you could help with.
- Inquire about the child's likes and dislikes.
- Check to see if you have the student's correct birthday because you would like to do something special that day.
- Let the family know that they are welcome to come to school and give them a time when you are available to visit with them.
- Give them information about when and how you can be contacted and ask the same of them.

The Follow-up After the Initial Contact

After you have made contact with the family and feel you have begun a relationship, you may be able to begin to focus on some school-oriented questions and information. This is the beginning of a communication flow. Begin with topics such as:

- the family's expectations of you, the school, and the child.
- the responsibilities the child has at home.
- how you manage your classroom.
- how you can help with the child's learning at home.

Besides information about their children and the classrooms, parents usually want to know:

- What is the policy on homework, discipline, attendance, and so forth?
- What is the cost for lunch and breakfast and how do you apply for reduced cost or free meals?
- Will my child be going on field trips?
- How are teachers and principals hired?
- Who decides on the curriculum?
- What extracurricular activities such as band, chorus, theater, and athletics are offered?
- What resources are available at the school such as nurses, guidance counselors, social workers, psychologists, and so on?

Do not expect to cover everything in one encounter. Remember that you can accomplish only so much with one letter, phone call, or home visit, especially with disconnected parents. Try to create the expectation that you will be communicating with the family on a regular basis through home visits, telephone calls, letters, and conferences.

Coordinating Resources and Services

Sometimes, telephone calls and home visits, usually one visit, allow you to informally assess the family's condition and need level. For example, during a home visit, you may become aware of family problems such as extreme poverty, drug abuse, alcoholism, child abuse, divorce, and teen pregnancy. When some trust is established between you and the parent, the school and community will be able to help by coordinating services and resources and providing information and support. (Coordinating Strategy best practices are presented in chapter 8.)

Connecting Letters

While providing some information, letters are primarily intended to overcome barriers and to begin building build trust and mutual respect. The letters should stress to the families that the faculty and staff feel that they are important and that the school cares. Use the guidelines presented at the beginning of this section when writing the letters. Additional suggestions include:

- Keep the letter short and to the point. Long letters are not very effective and some parents may have difficulty reading.
- Make sure the parents can read English. If not, write the letters in their native language.
- Emphasize how much you are looking forward to working with their child and the family.
- Let the family know they are welcome at school, and how to contact you for a visit.
- Encourage the family to contact you if they need information or have questions.

Connecting Telephone Calls

Positive telephone calls from school are not very common, especially to families with students at the middle and high school levels. Therefore, your call will come as a surprise to most of the families. If the parents feel disconnected from the school, the phone call may be viewed with some suspicion. Therefore, make sure telephone calls are upbeat.

With families that feel alienated and disenfranchised, a telephone call may not be enough to make a connection. A more intense one-on-one best practice like a home visit may be required.

The Connecting Home Visit

Home visits are probably the most effective best practice for making connections, especially with the most hard-to-reach parents. While time consuming and labor intensive, visiting families in their home is a strong indication of your concern, caring, and commitment. This personal one-on-one practice, if conducted properly, demonstrates that you want to work with the parents, as partners, to educate their children.

It would be great if all families were visited by someone from the school, especially the child's teacher. However, I recognize that conducting home visits is very labor intensive, so this intervention may have to be limited to the most disconnected families. However, I encourage you to extend this practice to as many of the families as possible.

It is very important to be clear about the intent of a home visit, especially when it is being used to connect with the families. The operative word for the visit is "collaboration." The objective is to make connections and to initiate a relationship that is based on trust, mutual respect, caring, and understanding. Therefore, the visitor's attitudes and assumptions about the families are crucial.

First, we must assume that most families are interested in their children's education and want them to succeed. Second, we must believe that under the right conditions most families are willing to work with the school. So, if the families are not involved and are missing, the reality may be that while there is a desire by the parents to be involved, certain barriers are preventing them from doing so. Consequently, the home visit is an important intervention strategy for beginning to overcome these barriers.

Families shouldn't feel that you have come to fix them. As we work with the families, we need to be careful not to, unintentionally, patronize or demean. All families, even the most distressed, have strengths. We must build on the strengths and attempt to eliminate the weaknesses. This can be tricky when the family is feeling alienated and disenfranchised from the school. However, it has been my experience that with a genuine caring effort, combined with perseverance, connections can be made and collaborative relationships can be established with most families.

Some may think that families, especially those with meager means, do not want faculty and staff coming to their home. I have found just the opposite. Most families, when approached in a helpful way, realize the school visitors are interested in them and their children. Actually, most families welcome and look forward to the visits. Once they get over the surprise of the school reaching out to them, family members seem to enjoy having teachers, counselors, and principals visit their homes.

When Are You Going to Visit My House?

I was working with the faculty at a school located in a distressed community in Nashville to determine the effects of home visits. The teachers were going to visit one half of the students' families. The half that was not visited would serve as the control group.

We quickly abandoned the study when the kids from the control group came to the school, all excited, and asking when the teachers were coming to visit them. Making connections and establishing relationships with the parents was far more important than the research, so the teachers made visits to the homes of all the students. We immediately scheduled home visits with all of the children. Even though we did not conduct the study, per se, the reactions of the kids who were not scheduled initially to be visited indicated the positive attitudes toward the home visits.

Planning and Conducting Home Visits

When planning for home visits, keep in mind parents are usually not accustomed to having teachers or family/school coordinators coming to their homes. Since nonthreatening visits from people in authority are not the norm, the visits must be personal and upbeat. Use the guidelines at the beginning of the chapter when deciding what information will be shared and what questions asked during the connecting visits. In addition to these important guidelines, the following are some suggestions for preparing and making home visits:

- If the family has a telephone, call to let them know that you would like to come by to get acquainted. Ask when it would be convenient to visit. Be flexible and adjust to the family's schedule when making the appointment.
- Mail or send appointment cards home with the child stating the date and time of the home visit. The mission statement, collective vision, or parent involvement slogan can be printed on the cards.
- Include a magnetic note holder when sending the out an appointment card or making a visit, so the family can post the information on the refrigerator door. Have positive messages printed on the note holders like those on the cards.
- Dress in good, but casual clothes when visiting the families. In the United States, strangers appearing in the neighborhood wearing formal business attire, especially in lower socioeconomic neighborhoods, are often perceived as threatening social agency officials or religious salespersons.
- If you are offered something to drink or eat, if at all possible, accept it. Refusing an offer of hospitality may send the wrong message.

- If you are uneasy about making the home visit because of the conditions in the community where the families live, it is a good idea to take someone with you and go during the daytime. Making a visit when you are anxious will not be as effective. Even though the families are living in a distressed community, most family members are law-abiding citizens and feel "caught" in these conditions.
- Wear an identification button or tag indicating who you are and what school or program you are with. The identification badges will let the families and neighbors know who you are and help them remember your name. Try not to make the tags too official or institutional.
- Have door hangers prepared with a message such as: "I came to visit you. Sorry that I missed you." Include your name and telephone number and ask the parent to call. The door hangers are used when you made an unscheduled stop and the family is not home, or if the family is not home for an appointment. Making connections with the family is sometimes difficult, so you need to use a positive approach and be persistent.
- Be aware of any language barriers. Bring a translator with you, if necessary, to facilitate communication.

Like with the telephone calls, once connections are made and relationships have begun, the home visits can focus on more parent education topics. For example, the family members can be shown how to read to their children and use home-learning activities. Some home visit programs lend or give books, educational toys, puzzles, games, and materials to the families. Again, be aware of any language barriers.

At a later home visit, the child's development in understanding and expressing language, use of small and large muscles, self-help and social skills, and so forth, can be assessed. An educational and social profile is constructed for the child that indicates strengths and weaknesses. The profile is used for designing appropriate learning strategies for the child at home and in school. Best practices for coaching the parents during home visits are described in chapter 9.

A Caution. Not all teachers and staff will perceive home visits as an opportunity to connect and work with the families. Some will be reluctant to visit the home and see them, at best, as a required inconvenience if forced to make them. I remember talking to a group of middle-school teachers and when I mentioned home visits their eyes rolled and glazed over. Making home visits in the middle school is not the norm. However, as tough as it may be to convince some teachers about the importance of connecting with the hard-to-reach parents, efforts must be made for the visits to occur.

Getting Ready to Reach Out and Connect

As stated in chapter 4, some of the barriers that prevent partnerships from forming between the families and the schools result from longstanding beliefs by the faculty and staff about the roles of parents, teachers, principals, and community members. That is, some teachers and administrators may not perceive that the school should be reaching out to the parents.

Therefore, in many schools, the faculty and staff will have to be convinced that by using the Self-Renewing Partnership Model to build collaborative relationships with the families their lives, and those of the children and parents, will be better. The following best practices are presented as ways to prepare the faculty and staff for this paradigm shift.

Family/school partnership planning sessions. One of the most effective ways to prepare and orient the faculty and staff to reach out to the families is for them to be involved in the development of the family/school partnership program. These sessions focus on such topics as: shared belief development, mission identification, goal setting, and intervention strategy selection. The participants need to decide "where they want to go" and "how to get there."

Need assessments. It is important to do your homework before attempting to reach out to the families. As part of the planning process, data are gathered to learn about family needs and self-interests, cultures, attitudes, and values. These can be gathered by surveying the families in person, by telephone, or asking them to respond to a questionnaire.

The need assessment can also identify barriers such as time, transportation, and child care constraints. The results of the need assessment are helpful when deciding on goals and objectives, and which intervention strategies are most likely to be most effective.

Family surveys. The survey questions evolve from the concepts underlying the family/school partnerships. The questions should be short, simple, and to the point. People usually do not respond to long, complicated surveys, whether in writing or verbally. If you use mailed surveys, make it as easy as possible to respond. Enclose a stamped envelope or construct the questionnaire in such a way that when completed, it can easily be folded and stapled together, and dropped in the mail. Another format is to use a postcard for a short survey. It is now possible to conduct a survey using computer software, but again, many hard-to-reach families do not have access to a computer or the skills to operate one.

Family interviews. Often the return rate from mailed surveys is low, especially with populations that feel disconnected. Therefore, instead of mailing the surveys to the families, data can be collected through parent interviews conducted at grocery and convenience stores or at open meetings in the neighborhood. If the school has a PTA/PTO and School Improvement Council, the members can be asked to help with the data collection.

The interview questions should try to identify both family strengths and weaknesses. If the family members are feeling alienated, it may be difficult to get much in-depth information, but it is a start. Even finding out if there is a psychological gap between the family and school is important information.

Family focus groups. To obtain information about family needs, desires, and culture, invite a small group of parents to breakfast, lunch, or for coffee to meet with the principal and one or two teachers. During the family focus group meetings, family members share their perspectives about their children, the school, and educational issues.

If the families are not comfortable about coming to school, or if it is inconvenient, the meetings can be held in the neighborhoods at community centers, churches, businesses, and similar locations. Once the families feel connected, the family members may want to meet at the school occasionally, or on a regular basis. Try to respond to the families' desires about location and times. The intent is to gather information, but it is also a way for the families to feel connected and to want to be involved with the school.

Neighborhood bus tours. In some settings, faculty and staff are not familiar with the environments where the families live. Sometimes the teachers have never been in their students' neighborhoods.

To prepare teachers to reach out to the families, organize school bus tours of the neighborhoods. The tours can be scheduled during workdays or just before the children arrive to begin the school year. The tours can be part of the teachers' in-service training. The bus rides are a way to increase awareness and understanding, and provide new perspectives about the students and their families. The bus tours can begin to answer such questions as:

- What are family's and children's views of the world?
- How do the families live?
- What do the children do in the neighborhood?
- What are the kids good at?

After the bus tour, a debriefing session is conducted so the participants can share their perceptions, raise questions, and make suggestions for additional connecting plans. Later, more intensive best practices, such as neighborhood forums, and home visits, can be used to make connections and gain a more in-depth understanding about the families.

The deluxe neighborhood tour. A way to make the tour of the neighborhood even more effective is to include a luncheon with some of the family members. Contact the local clergy and see if they would be willing to host a luncheon for the teachers and some of the families in their neighborhood. By having a meal together, teachers and parents will have an opportunity to get to know each another, ask questions, and make connections. The cost of luncheons can be covered by donations, grants, neighborhood groups or the school district.

Community walk. If the most of school's families live close by, you can organize a community walk. The added benefit of this type of tour is opportunity to interact with the community members such as parents, neighbors, shop owners, and clergy as are walking through the neighborhood.

Parent involvement conference. Organize a conference for family leaders, teachers, counselors, and administrators to discuss ways to create family/school partnerships. Spotlight successful family involvement practices operating in other schools to help stimulate action.

COMMUNICATING: BUILDING ON THE CONNECTING STRATEGY

The best practices presented in this chapter are implemented to overcome barriers and make connections. Once connections are made, the focus shifts to establishing two-way communication flows between the families and the school. The programs, activities, and events described in the following chapter are ways that the school can form the communication flows.

Chapter 7

Communicating: Establishing a Flow

Table 7.1

Connecting	Communicating	Coordinating	Coaching

You know the "uh oh" feeling you get when you look in the mailbox and find a letter from the Internal Revenue Service (IRS). Unfortunately, many people get that same sinking sensation when an unexpected letter arrives from their child's school. The reason for this negative reaction is that communications from the school typically range from cool and impersonal, to negative and threatening. This may be what is occurring now, but it doesn't have to be this way.

It is overly optimistic to expect that we will have warm feelings toward the IRS, even if they start sending out thank-you notes. However, I do believe the "oh good" reactions can replace the "uh oh" responses we have toward school correspondence. This will happen if two-way communication flows that emphasize the positive are established between the school and the families.

Certainly, all communications between the school and the families cannot be positive. At times, there will be problems and concerns that have to be addressed. However, if collaborative relationships built on positive communications are in place, when problems do occur, they are more likely to be resolved in a positive manner. Information is the currency of power, and the sharing of power builds relationships.

Trusting relationships between the families and the school will be the foundation for problem-solving where the teachers support families, rather than blame. And, the parents will be doing likewise. By working together, the parents will feel like insiders rather than outsiders in the educational process.

Parents want to know what is happening in school and how their child is progressing. While being as positive as possible, it is important for the school to be honest and tell it like it is. The families want specific information about how they can help at school and at home. It is important for the families to learn how the operation of the school works, so they can plug in and be partners.

Not surprising, many years ago, Jane C. Lindle (1989) found that the most enhancing factor in home/school relationships was the personal touch (when teachers and principals take a personal interest in their children).

As discussed in the previous chapter, families must be connected with the school before the parties can communicate effectively. Connecting best practices are used to reach out to begin building relationships. After these connections are made, communicating best practices are employed to establish a two-way communication flow and to strengthen collaborative relationships between the school and the families. Once a collaborative relationship is developed and a two-way communication flow established, the school can implement the Coaching Strategy to enhance the families' ability and willingness to play the Parent Partner Roles.

Therefore, the Communicating Strategy is designed to do the following:

- establish two-way communication flows between the families and the school
- continue to build collaborative relationships with the families
- begin to increase family and community support for the school's programs and activities

COMMUNICATING BEST PRACTICES

The programs, activities, and events presented in this chapter focus on ways to establish effective two-way communication between the families and the school. However, many of these best practices can also improve communications between parents and children, and teachers and students. For a family/school partnership to be effective, there needs to be good communication between all parties.

Depending upon the family and school situations, establishing a two-way communication flow can be fairly easy, or very difficult. As argued in the previous chapter, there needs to be a connection between the families and school to have a communication flow. The families will vary in how much they feel connected with the school. Some parents will be very comfortable with the school, while others are only connected in a marginal way.

Therefore, the kind and magnitude of communicating best practices that the school decides to implement will depend on the degree to which the targeted family population is connected. Consequently, some programs and activities are focused, while others are very broad.

Because the connecting process blends into the communicating process, some best practices overlap. Some are similar in format, but differ in intent and emphasis. For example, best practices for making the school more user-friendly are good connectors with the families, but the programs and activities are ongoing since a welcoming school is an asset in building partnerships.

The following sections describe best practices that can be used to implement the Communicating Strategy. The best practices are grouped by the following categories: communicating in writing, telephone and electronic communicating, face-to-face communicating, group communicating, and mass communicating.

Communicating in Writing

Analyzing Current Best Practices

Before deciding on what new best practices to use, it is a good idea to review what is currently in use. Gather copies of letters, notices, newsletters, bulletins, e-mails, and other written materials that have gone out to the families during the past year. Examine them carefully to ascertain the nature, quantity, and quality of the communications. Look not only at what is written, but also for how the message is stated—the tone and clarity.

Written messages to the families need to be as positive as possible, communicating respect, trust, and caring. All too often correspondence from the school talks down to the families and students, or is sterile and impersonal. The school should want the parents to be partners; therefore, the communications should express this desire. Ask yourself, "Are current written communications helpful, informative, and respectful?" and "Will families know that the school wants to work with them to educate their children?"

The correspondences should be void of educational jargon and be written as simply as possible. This is a good general writing rule, but it is especially important in this case because some parents may have difficulty reading. If English is the second language for a segment of your population, write a version of the materials using the families' native language. This is a major issue for some schools. I visited a school district in Los Angeles where newsletters were written in 17 different languages.

Welcoming letters. Before school starts, or early in the school year, have the teachers and principal send letters to the students and families. The purpose of these letters is to welcome the students and families to the learning community and to establish or build the two-way communication flows. While providing some information, this practice is primarily intended to continue building trust and mutual respect.

The letters show the families that the faculty and staff feel they are important and the school cares. As mentioned before, for those families that do not feel connected with the school, the letters may not be very effective. For these hard-to-reach parents, more intensive one-on-one best practices such as connecting telephone calls or home visits may be required to make a connection (see chapter 6 for a discussion of these best practices).

The following are some guidelines for composing welcoming letters:

- Keep the letters short and to the point.
- State how much you are looking forward to working with the families and their children.
- Let the families know they are welcome at school and how to arrange for a visit.
- Encourage the families to ask if they need information or have questions. Let them know when and how to contact you.

Sending out these welcoming letters can set a positive tone for the whole year. They are very helpful as you reach out to create partnerships with the families.

Welcome cards. Instead of letters, welcome back cards can be used. These cards have positive and inviting messages printed on them, and principals and/or the teachers sign them before they are sent to the students and families. While not as personalized as the letters, they are efficient, especially when you have large numbers of students.

Positive notes. During the year, make it a regular practice to send the families positive personalized notes about their children's progress, behavior, and activities. Sending positive notes should be a continuous activity, not a one-shot deal. Reach an agreement among teachers, principals, and counselors, by consensus if possible, on how many positive notes will be sent per week, or per month. I believe a parent should receive a positive note about their child at least once a month.

Obviously, because of the large number of students that each middle- and high-school teacher works with, it is easier to send more notes in the elementary schools. However, when a parent receives a positive note from a teacher about their high-school or middle-school student, it is a wonderful surprise. To make it easier for each teacher, the faculty can rotate which class or group of students they will be responsible for at different times during the year. Some schools use parent volunteers to help organize and mail the notes; however, the teachers still write the notes.

Happygrams or success cards. "Success cards" or "happygrams" are stamped postcards that the teachers use to write the positive notes. The cards have the school name, mascot, or the partnership theme printed on them with a space for a brief message. To help the teachers, the cards are placed in a container in the school office and the staff mails them. While the cards are less personal than the handwritten notes, the convenience is a plus for the teachers. The important thing is that a positive note goes home to all families.

Refrigerator Door Culture

By looking at the refrigerator door you can usually learn a lot about the culture of the family. The refrigerator door is a common spot for displaying photographs of family members, friends, and relatives; schedules of special events like concerts, recitals, and sporting events; awards; and other keep-sakes. All too often, there is nothing positive from the school related to the child's learning activities such as positive notes from teachers and examples of school work and children's art.

Wouldn't it be nice if the school's mission or philosophy was posted on the door as well? Bulletin boards can be used when the refrigerator door is covered. Having too many positive things to display would be a great problem to have.

Partnership magnetic note holders. Magnetic note holders can be used to help build the refrigerator door culture. Each family receives a special partnership note holder to post messages, student papers and pictures, invitations, and announcements from school.

The note holders are sent home with a positive note or given out at school meetings, conferences, and home visits. The families are told to expect that positive things will follow. The note holders are shaped like chalkboards or apples and are inscribed with upbeat messages such as:

- What's happening in school!
- Good news from school!
- Look what I did at school this week!

Use of logos and mascots. Most families and students identify with the school's logo or mascot. By placing the logo or picture of the mascot on all positive and upbeat communications, the parents recognize that the letter or note is from school and look forward to the correspondence. A logo representing the family/school/community partnership (e.g., hands joining together, an apple, etc.) can be created and used on the communications. These symbols are especially important when attempting to develop a positive communication system.

Vision statements. When a collective vision for a family/school is decided upon, place it on all school correspondence (e.g., caring and sharing, education is a family affair, etc.). Display the vision on sweatshirts, banners, coffee mugs, glasses, and posters. It is important to promote the partnership between the families and school.

Friday folders. In elementary and middle schools, a good practice for keeping the family informed about the child's progress is to send home a Friday folder containing the child's work for the week. Student papers, projects, and art work are great communication links. Provide each child with a heavy-duty file folder or large, clasp envelope that can be used as the Friday folder. Get the children involved by having them label and decorate their folders.

Each week, include a comment or suggestion sheet with a place for the parent to sign. Ask the parent to sign the sheet and send it back with the child on Monday. Remember, children are not always the most reliable carriers of information. If the use of Friday folders is a regular practice, ask the parents to call the school if a folder does not arrive home with the child.

Signal stamps. Provide the teachers with rubber stamps to use on papers that they send home. Messages like "parents make it happen" or "working together" are stamped on the students' papers to signal the parents that they should look at it carefully. The stamps are used both to indicate outstanding work and to signal papers that need some parent attention for other reasons.

Teachergrams. Use teachergrams to maintain regular two-way communications with the family about the child's progress, activities, and special events. The teachergrams are produced in a "half and half" format. The teachers use the top half for their message, whereas, the bottom half is used for the parents' responses, comments, suggestions, and questions.

The teachergrams can be printed as a two-page form using carbonless copy paper for the top page. When the teacher writes the message to the family on the top sheet, the message is copied on the bottom page. The teacher sends the original and keeps the copy for his or her files.

Interactive homework. Homework is a fundamental aspect of a student's academic development. Research results have repeatedly shown a direct positive correlation between homework and achievement scores, especially if teachers consistently grade and comment on the assignments.

In addition to improving academic performance, parents, teachers, and principals view homework as a tool for developing self-discipline, responsibility, and study habits. Homework should be an interactive activity that provides opportunities for continuous two-way communication flows between the families and school.

Homework should have a definite and valid purpose and assignments must be clear. The assignments can create or reinforce positive or negative feelings about school and teachers, so the work must be meaningful.

It is important to let parents know how and when to help the child with homework. Encourage the family to establish a good home-learning environment with regular times for doing homework. Homework should be a part of the family's lifestyle. Separate homework from home-learning activities. The two activities are related, but each has slightly different purposes.

Homework is designed to strengthen and increase the skills and knowledge presented in the classroom. Home-learning activities enhance, reinforce, and expand the school's curriculum. The family should always be looking for "teachable moments"—situations and events that will help the child. For example, putting groceries and supplies away provides a time when parent and child can interact by reading labels, discussing sources of food, and investigating weights and measurements.

The parents should work with the teacher to coordinate the child's classroom work and homework with the home-learning activities. It is a good idea for the teachers, especially middle-school and high-school teachers, to send families information about their course curricula, policies, and expectations about homework, how they can be contacted and ways they can help the students.

TIPS

Dr. Joyce Epstein of John Hopkins University has developed a program called Teachers Involved Parents in Schoolwork (TIPS). The program is designed to involve parents in the children's homework and learning activities. The interactive and hands-on activities are correlated with the school's curriculum and focus on specific skills in language arts, science, and math. The idea is for the families, school, and children to work together and to make homework meaningful and an enjoyable aspect of family life.

Weekly assignment sheets. Some schools send home assignment sheets that list the students' assignments for the week. In a self-contained class, the assignments can be listed by subject on one sheet. In secondary schools, where the students change classes, a separate sheet can be produced for each subject, or each teacher can record his or her assignments on one calendar.

This practice is helpful, but time consuming. It may be necessary to be selective and prepare sheets only for those students who are having difficulties getting their assignments completed. It is important to coordinate the assignments among several teachers.

Some schools have websites, where teachers can post assignments and have e-mails so students can ask questions and get information. This works well where the families have access to computers and are comfortable using the computers. With hard-to-reach families, the assignments sheets may have to send home using nonelectronic means.

Progress reports. Student progress reports are sent to the families on a regular basis. All students receive all reports, not just those who are having difficulty. This is a good way to let the families know how their children are doing in school and it sends a positive message about the students that are doing well.

The reports are sent at a set time (e.g., first three weeks of a semester). When this practice is built into the school's schedule, the families will know when to expect the reports and can notify the school if they do not receive one.

Red Flags

If a student is having severe difficulties with a class or subject and is in danger of failing, it is important to call the parent immediately, rather than wait for progress report time. The parents are partners with the school and need to be informed right away about any problems their child is having. Failing to let the families know about any major difficulties the student is having with school work, behavior, or attendance is a cardinal sin.

Home study prescriptions. A family resource center in Wichita, Kansas, uses a clever format to inform parents of areas where the child needs help. Forms that resemble medical prescriptions sheets are used to indicate specific skills to be worked on at home (e.g., reading, math, basic skills, etc.). The teachers determine the skills that are lacking in the classrooms, or in some cases, the needed skills are identified in a math or reading lab. Copies are given to everyone involved.

Report card instructions. When sending out report cards, include a sheet of instructions on how to read and interpret the card. Explain the grading system and define any symbols and codes. Also indicate how the families can receive more information and ask questions.

Noncustodial Parents

Many children live with a single parent, or in a blended family, and have a noncustodial parent living elsewhere. It is important to keep the noncustodial parent involved. If there is not a legal restraint, noncustodial parents' names and addresses are placed on the schools' mailing lists so they receive progress reports, report cards, newsletters, positive notes, and announcements.

Parent policy handbook. Publish a parent handbook that includes such items as school rules and policies; visiting and volunteer opportunities; telephone numbers of teachers, guidance counselors, and principals; a description of the curriculum, grade-level learning goals and objectives; and a summary of extracurricular activities.

Newsletters. Send a weekly or monthly newsletter to the families and community groups with copies to local newspaper editors and radio station managers. A variety of information can be contained, such as what the children are doing in school, ideas for special projects, reports of joint or individual accomplishments, student art work, announcements, and invitations to come to school for lunch. Before grades are posted, also include an explanation on how to read a report card, and who and where to call if the family has questions or needs more information.

Include such things as a parent education section and a student column that features fun home-learning activities, games, jokes, and so on. List resources such as books, pamphlets, videos, cassettes, and software that are available in the school library or family room.

A mini-survey may be enclosed in each newsletter asking for information, suggestions, comments, and concerns. Data on special topics such as discipline, drug and alcohol abuse, teenage pregnancy, homework, the arts, and adult education are gathered. The survey has a tear-off response sheet with a return mailing stamp.

With the advent of desktop publishing, the newsletter can be enhanced with graphics and photographs. Students can be invited to contribute, or a class can be asked to produce the whole issue as a special project. In many schools, several versions of the newsletters are needed so that they are available in the language used at home.

Yearly calendars. A calendar is a good means of keeping the families and community appraised of the school's program and activities. The calendars can also serve as thank-you gifts. Two popular formats are the wall calendar and the pocket appointment book. Each year, the school publishes the calendars and mails or gives them to parents and community members at meetings and home visits. The school's collective vision or mission statement is displayed on the cover or top of the calendar. The calendar also lists school personnel and telephone numbers.

The calendar outlines the school year and shows when special activities and events are scheduled. Besides holidays, teacher work days, and vacation times, the calendar shows the times and dates for parent-teacher conferences, PTA/PTO meetings, social and cultural events, marking periods, progress reports, report cards, and similar events. Also included are schedules for athletics, drama and music events, science fairs, and other school activities. As a special touch, the students' birthdays may be listed. Suggestions for helping children at home with homework or learning activities and other ways to be involved can also be inserted throughout the calendar.

Weekly event flyers. One-page flyers updating families and the community on events and activities scheduled for the upcoming week, new happenings, special programs and sports results are published each week. The event and activity sheets are sent home with the students, mailed to the families, and distributed at grocery stores, churches, service clubs, and so forth.

Monthly calendars. Another variation is to produce a calendar for each month, which then is mailed to the families at the end of the current month. The monthly calendars are up-to-date on meetings and programs, and they are opportunities to remind the families about special events. With the widespread availability of desktop publishing, this approach is both practical and economical.

Parent bookmarks. A simple way to help motivate parents to play their partner roles is to give them specially made bookmarks as gifts. The bookmarks can be made by hand and decorated or produced with a computer. The bookmarks are made out of heavy paper and are laminated so they will last.

Examples of messages that can be placed on the bookmarks include:

- Parents are the child's first and most important teacher
- Parents share with their children what they have learned . . . and the children's lives become richer because of it
- Education is a family affair

How are we doing surveys. After the first few weeks of each semester, the principal and/or the teachers send a letter to the families asking two important questions:

- How is your child doing in our school?
- Is there anything we can do to make it better?

A self-addressed, stamped envelope is enclosed for convenience and to get a greater response. While this adds to the cost, the stamped envelope conveys the importance you place on the families' comments, suggestions, and opinions.

Annual school reports. Each year, publish an annual report that describes student outcomes, school achievements, and partnership activities. Included in the report are such items as overall achievement scores; attendance figures; honors and awards earned by students, faculty, parents, and community members; and special programs and activities. The annual report is an opportunity to celebrate the past year's successes.

Thank-you and appreciation notes. At every opportunity, send thank-you and appreciation notes to parents, community members, faculty, and staff who contribute to the family/school partnership's mission. For example, appreciation notes are sent to parents for volunteering and supporting the school, working with children at home, going on a field trip with their child's class, participating in a reading program, providing enrichment experiences for their child, and so forth.

The school or project's name and logo are printed across the top of the notes and on the envelopes. The collective vision or mission statement can also be displayed.

You probably cannot overdo this best practice. People want and need to be appreciated and recognized.

Partnership request and message bulletin boards. Bulletin boards are placed outside the classrooms and/or family room for teachers and parents to leave messages, make requests, and share items of interest. Teachers can make requests for inexpensive items needed for the classroom such as tin cans, paper bags, egg cartons, paper rolls, string, newspapers, magazines, soil, boxes, and so on. The families use the board to announce meetings, share parenting ideas, list items for sale, and seek babysitting and day care. Remember to write the messages in various languages if needed.

Telephone and Electronic Communicating

Cell phones, computers, smart phones, and other electronic devices have revolutionized how we communicate personally and in the business world. The schools are now beginning to take advantage of this technology. There are a variety of options for reaching out and communicating with the families. These best practices are described and discussed in this section.

The telephone, of course, is not a new innovation, but the use of the phone to build partnerships is not a common practice. As noted earlier, the welcoming telephone call is an excellent means of strengthening the connections between the school and the families and to establish collaborative relationship. Guidelines for planning and making welcoming telephone calls are presented in the following special section.

The welcoming telephone call. As with the welcoming letter, the purpose of the welcoming telephone call is to establish or strengthen a two-way communication flow and to build the collaborative relationship between the family and the school. The difference between a connecting and a welcoming telephone call is more a matter of emphasis of content than process.

The intent of the connecting call is to overcome any barriers that might exist between the families and the school; whereas, the welcoming telephone call focuses on building relationships with families that are already connected. Besides welcoming the parents and students to the learning community, the calls provide information and respond to questions.

Both the connecting and the communicating calls should be positive and upbeat; with the overall goal of building partnerships between the families and the school. The types and amount of information provided and the kinds of questions asked during the calls will depend upon the nature of the connection with each family.

When preparing to make welcoming calls, it is a good idea to review the guidelines for making connecting telephone calls that are provided in chapter 6. Most of the connecting suggestions can be used when planning communicating telephone call.

Telephone and Internet Technology

As stated, combining telephone technology with other electronic programs has revolutionized the communication process. Through the use of technology, many options such as voice and e-mail, the Internet, faxes, answering machines, and other computer programs are used to improve the communication flows between the school and families.

This technology is particularly useful in rural communities where families are separated by great distances. The technology can also be helpful to parents with unusual time constraints. However, recent studies indicate only 40 percent of the population have access to the Internet. I suspect many of the 60 percent that don't have access are part of the hard-to-reach parent population.

Examples of telephone technology best practices include:

- Teacher voice mail—The school establishes a voice mail system for the teachers and other staff members. Parents and students can call and leave a message. Teachers can place informational messages on the system for the families.
- Teacher e-mail—Similar to the voice mail, an e-mail system is established for the teachers and other staff members. Parents and students can e-mail the teachers for information and to ask questions.
- Websites—The school's website includes a system for the teachers and staff to place information such as assignments, meetings, activities, and such for the families. Again, a caution, don't rely only on this means because many families are not computer savvy.
- Attendance hotline—Student absences for the day are placed on the telephone and e-mail system each day so the parents can call and check on their child. A computer program can be installed that automatically calls to the student's home when the child is absent. A difficulty with the technology is that with so many parents working outside the home, the students may get home and erase the message before the parents can hear it. The opportunity for the parent to call in and get the absentee list helps to alleviate this problem.

- Homework hotline—This program operates in the late afternoons and evenings. The hotline is operated by teachers, aides, students, parents, or community members. Students call to ask questions and get help with homework.
- Parent hotline—This program is similar to the homework hotline, except it is a service for family members. They can call in for advice on parenting issues, education concerns, and so on.
- Assignment hotline—This is a voice mail system where parents and students can get homework assignments. The teachers place their assignments on the system at the end of the day or for the week. The assignments can also be placed on the school's website or e-mail. The e-mail system can be set up for the families to leave messages for the teachers.
- 24-hour school announcement line—Parents and students are able to get recorded school announcements such as event schedules and school closing. The callers are able to choose from a selection of messages about parenting and educational issues.

Telephone trees. Establish a telephone network so families can be contacted without placing the burden on any one parent. One parent calls five parents and each of those five call five more, and so on. Make sure the callers are capable of conversing in the language spoken in the homes they are assigned to call.

The telephone tree allows families to be notified quickly in case of changes in meeting times, early dismissals and closings due to weather, advance announcements of special events and programs, and similar news. The network can be used to ask parents if they would be able to help with field trips and other activities, provide materials for special projects, and assist new families in adjusting to the community. When possible, have both the landline and cell phone numbers available.

Parent attendance telephone committee. Parent volunteers are organized to make calls to the homes of students who are absent. Telephone calls are also made to families of students who have been tardy several times. The parent volunteers are from different attendance areas so that they are familiar with the family cultures and languages in the neighborhood.

Again, try to have both the landline and cell phone numbers for the parents. There are software programs available that allow the school to automatically call the parents' homes when a student is absent. These automated programs are fine, but having a real person making the call is much better.

TV parent hour. Some school districts produce a regularly scheduled television program that deals with issues of interest to parents. Some cities have their own public channel. The "Parent Hour" program can consist of interviews, call-in sessions, student presentations, and training sessions on parenting issues. Shows are staffed by teachers, administrators, counselors, students, and volunteers.

School video loan libraries. Videotape student performances such as athletic contests, plays, band and chorus concerts, dance recitals; classroom and holiday activities; parent meeting and training sessions; and other events and activities and make them available to families. Copies of the tapes are lent to the families to view or copy at home. CDs can also be burned for the parents if the technology is available.

The parents are notified what tapes or CDs are available. The CDs need to be available in different languages if needed.

Face-to-Face Communicating

Telephoning, e-mailing, video teleconferencing, and other technologies are great, but face-to-face is the most effective means of communicating, especially with hard-to-reach families. When attempting to form collaborative relationships, teachers, principals, and other school personnel must find ways to interact personally with the parents. The best practices in this section present different ways the school can reach out to communicate with the families.

The parent-teacher conference is one of the most common face-to-face communicating activities in the school. However, many times this practice does not foster partnerships with the families. Guidelines are presented for planning and conducting parent-teacher conferences so that they improve communications and build collaborative relationships between the school and the families.

Meetings with teachers. Let the families know when parents can come to school and meet with different teachers. Sometimes, certain planning period times work or at other times, monthly or bimonthly evening times may need to be established. Communicate the available times by means of letters to the parents, e-mails, newsletters, websites, and such.

Family corners. A corner in the classrooms can be set up for family members to visit and observe the lessons and activities in the classroom. The area should have a comfortable adult-sized chair or rocking chair and a table to write on. Observing the classroom helps the parents to understand what the children are learning and how they are being taught. Information related to the school day and the curriculum can also be available in the "corner."

Visits such as these increase communications and help the family members become better partners. The family corners are also good places for a parent of a disruptive child to come to school for a couple days to observe the student.

Interaction contact points. Establish a routine of being available to greet and talk with parents at typical school contact locations, such as bus stops, student drop-off and pick-up locations, and school campus entrances. Soon, families will get used to having a short conversation when dropping off or picking up a child. These informal encounters are opportunities to share successes and concerns, and ask for information. The interactions lay a foundation for other partnership activities. I can't overemphasize how important these informal communications were for me when I was a school principal.

Significant person. Make sure that each child is known well by at least one person in the school and let the parent know who that person is and how to contact him or her. With this connection, the student always has someone who can help if he or she is having a problem or concern. When I was a high school principal, I often ended up being quite close to the students who were sent to my office for disciplinary reasons. They gravitated toward me when they realized I was someone who cared.

Neighborhood walks. Walk through the neighborhoods on a Saturday once a month to meet and chat with the parents. These walks will give you a feel for how the families live. The frequency of the walks will depend on how well the school and the families are communicating.

Clowning Around

In an effort to reach out and communicate with some hard-to-reach families, the faculty at a school in Nashville dressed up as clowns and rode through a low-income housing development that surrounded the school in the back of decorated pickup trucks. They held up signs and gave out pamphlets about the preschool and parent involvement program that was being started. As they drove through the neighborhood, they gave the children and family members candy, balloons, and other goodies.

The school contacted the families' favorite radio station and asked if they would parade with the teachers in their marketing van. Music and messages about the new program were broadcast over the van's loud speakers. Hearing the music, the family came out to the street to see the clowns.

Most radio stations are willing to participate with their van in other events, such as family picnics, school festivals, and school registrations. This provides a service to the school and gives the station exposure.

Saturday question and answer sessions. Set up information tables at specific locations in the community where people gather (e.g., grocery stores, recreation centers, department stores, union halls, churches, parks, etc.). Encourage the parents to sit for a moment and ask questions about the school. Ask the families about their children.

Clergy power. Contact members of the clergy and inquire if you may speak to the congregations about how they can get involved with the education of the children. Keep clergy informed by sending copies of newsletter, announcements, policy handbooks, resources and services directories, and so on.

Community leaders and other powerbrokers. Locate community leaders, politicians, athletics, and others, and ask them to help you by communicating with the families and encouraging them to be involved with the schools. The community leaders can form a neighborhood connection network to talk about programs, activities, concerns, suggestions, and needs.

Working with immigrant populations. Families that use English as a second language may need special help integrating into the learning community. Some schools hire outreach staff members who speak the families' language to make home visits to build relationship and talk about the importance of involvement and listen to family concerns. The staff also speaks to groups in the neighborhood at church, synagogue, and other community meetings.

Parent/Teacher Conferences

As mentioned, conferences between the parent and teacher, and sometimes the parent, teacher, and student, are some of the most common and important communicating events. Face-to-face interaction is potentially a very effective form of communication, especially for problem-solving. However, to reach their potential, conferences must be planned and conducted in a manner consistent with the partnership philosophy.

Historically, most parent/teacher conferences occur in the elementary grades. The frequency and number of conferences taper off in the middle grades, and then again in the upper grades. This is not surprising since parent involvement activities in middle and high schools have traditionally been less extensive. Naturally, I believe the norms need to change so there are strong family/school partnership activities in all schools.

There are two general types of parent-teacher conferences, which have different, but interrelated functions. The purpose of the typical parent/teacher conference should be to discuss the child's progress and activity at school and at home and to explore ways to enhance the child's academic and social development. Conferences are routinely scheduled once or twice a year. The purpose of the second type of conference is to deal with a particular issue, problem, or concern. The latter, is held on demand by the school or the family.

Sometimes, of course, conferences can end up serving both functions. Both types of conferences should be seen as opportunities to build the partnership between the school and the family. However, if they are not planned, organized, and conducted properly, the meetings, particularly the second type, can have negative effect on relationships.

Like other best practices, it is crucial that all parties enter into the dialogues with appropriate attitudes and expectations. The conferences should be characterized by positive constructive two-way sharing of information, assessment, problem-solving, planning, feedback, and suggestions. For the conferences to be the most effective, the family and the school need to be connected and communicating. However, if this is not the case, conferences, especially the first type, should be approached as an event designed to reach out to the families and build relationships.

Typical Conferences

Planning the Conference

The following are some guidelines for a typical parent/teacher conference:

- When scheduling the conference, inform the parent and child of your expectations and perceptions concerning the purpose of the conference. Recognize that some parents (and the children) may be apprehensive about the meeting. Assure them that you want the conference to be a positive experience for everyone.
- If you think it is appropriate, ask the parents if they would like the child to attend the meeting. Whether the child attends or not, both the teacher and parent should discuss the purpose of the conference with the child before the meeting. After the meeting, encourage the family member to talk with the child about what happened at the conference. You should discuss the meeting with the child as well.
- Suggest to the parents that they prepare questions to be asked at the conference. Provide sample questions such as:
  - How is my child progressing with his or her school work?
  - What are my child's strengths and weaknesses?
  - How does my child interact with classmates?
  - Does my child take part in group projects and discussions?
  - How often will my child have homework?
  - What kind of homework will he or she have?
  - How can I help with homework?
  - Are there regularly scheduled tests?
  - How can I help my child prepare for them?
  - What textbooks is my child using?
  - Are there any supplies or materials that I need to have available?

- Send a list of potential topics for discussion. School-directed topics include:
  - curriculum and course content
  - services and programs offered by school
  - grading procedures
  - standardized test programs
  - extracurricular activities
  - discipline policies
- Child-directed topics might include:
  - any special health needs or problem
  - outside interests and hobbies
  - feelings about school
  - relationships with brothers and sisters
- Ask the parent to prepare a list of the child's strengths and weaknesses based on their observations.
- Ask the parent to bring any relevant medical information such as allergies; vision, speech, or hearing problems; and so on.
- Organize a folder with examples of the student's work, test results, and any notes or questions from the parent.
- Prepare an agenda for the conference. Decide what strengths and weaknesses to share and what information you need from the parent. Identify potential areas to be included in a collaborative action plan between the families and school.
- Identify and inform the families of any concerns or issues you may have before the conference so they can be prepared.
- Eliminate any logistical barriers that might prevent the parents from participating and create a welcoming environment for the family.
- Be aware of family schedules, factory shifts, church meetings, distance, and so on, when deciding on the days, times, and locations for the conferences. Be flexible in scheduling meetings, such as mornings, afternoons, and evenings. Some schools hold conferences on Saturdays. Teachers should be compensated for the evening or Saturday work with a scheduled day off during the week or extended vacation time.
- Be sensitive to language and cultural differences. Make contact in the home language, and have interpreters available at the conference if the family does not speak fluent English. Asking a parent volunteer from the neighborhood to serve as a translator can make the family more comfortable with the process.
- Have students write and send letters to their parents inviting them to attend the conference.
- Place the dates and schedules on the school's website.

- Collaborate with other staff members to design and print special conference invitations for everyone's use.
- Have childcare available, especially for single parents.
- Make plans to provide transportation to and from the conference, if no other way is available.
- Hold some conferences in the neighborhoods. This is an especially good idea if the families are not well connected with the school. This way, the parents and teachers can meet on the families' home territory.
- If the conferences are being held in the classroom, arrange a seating area outside the room where the parents can wait. Hold the meetings away from the door so you and the parent can have some privacy. Have adult-size chairs available for the conference and in the waiting area. Avoid having a desk or table separating you and the parent. Having coffee, tea, and light refreshments available can help set a positive tone for the conference.

Conducting the Conference

- Hold the meeting in a comfortable place where there is privacy so the discussion won't be overheard.
- Before beginning the dialogue, review with the parents (or parent and student) the purpose of the conference and let them know, again, that you wish the meeting to be a positive experience for everyone.
- Inform the family that you consider the conference to be a meeting between equal partners. Always be careful not to patronize, demean, or lecture the parent or child.
- Conduct the conference with mutual respect and caring for all parties. Concerns, opinions, and suggestions should be shared openly and honestly.
- Be aware that you are a significant person in the life of the child and the family. Choose your words carefully because what you say will have an impact (positive or negative) on the family.
- Avoid using education jargon. Let the parents know it is appropriate to ask you to explain any terms or concepts that they do not understand.
- Describe the school's expectations of the parents, and explain what the parents can expect from you. Ask for comments and suggestions.
- Be clear about the time available for the conference. Let the parent know that another meeting can be scheduled if more time is needed.
- Share your agenda and ask the parent for additions. Encourage the parent to take notes.
- Discuss the student's progress in your class, focusing on what has been learned since school started. Talk about areas of growth. Ask the parents how they feel the child has progressed and if they have any concerns.

- Describe the child's strengths and weaknesses, beginning with the strengths. Ask the parents to share their list of the child's strength and weaknesses based on their observations.
- Discuss areas of strength as well as areas that need improvement. Ask the parent for comments, suggestions, or concerns.
- Discuss how you and the family will work together to reinforce the strengths and address the areas needing improvement. Describe any additional programs, services, and resources that are available to the child and parent.
- Develop a collaborative action plan and reach consensus on any steps that need to be taken to enhance the child's academic and social development both at home and at school.
- Identify how you and the parent will to implement the plan.
- Present ways the parent can help at home. Prepare a parent worksheet that describes activities that the parent and child can do.
- Suggest the parents maintain a file of their child's school work, outside projects, and activities.
- If appropriate, initiate a learning contract between the child, parent, and teacher that outlines responsibilities and goals for all parties.
- End the conference by summarizing the child's strengths, areas for growth, and the action plan. Describe and discuss any follow-up procedures that are appropriate.

Follow-up to the Conference

- Make a follow-up phone call or send a note or letter. Let the parents know how much you appreciate their involvement and how important it is to the child. Ask if they have any questions or concerns.
- Provide a feedback form that parents can use when they have questions or concerns.
- If appropriate, send a summary of the collaborative action plan. Telephone the parent, two to four weeks later, to check on the progress and plan the next step.
- If the child did not attended the conference, find a time where both the teacher and parent can review with the child the outcome of the conference and the action plan.
- Share the outcomes of the conference with other school personnel if needed.
- Have the students write notes to the parents thanking them for participating in the conferences.
- Recognize the parents' participation in the conferences in the school newsletter and/or over the school intercom.

- Hold end-of-the-year parent recognition ceremonies with awards, door prizes, and refreshments.

Problem-solving Conference

Creating and maintaining a positive atmosphere can be difficult with this type of conference. When a meeting is scheduled by the parents or the school because the child is having difficulties, it is possible that the family, and maybe the teacher, will arrive at the meeting upset and angry. The parents may blame the school for the problem, and the teacher may be ready to blame the parents.

Even in the most difficult encounters, the intent should still be to move the issue from a win-lose to a win-win decision-making approach. By using a problem-solving approach, the conference will more likely have positive outcomes for everyone.

The dynamics of a problem-solving conference can be different from the typical meeting. These differences influence the way the meetings are planned and conducted. For example, when conducting the problem-solving conference, it is very important that those involved (e.g., teachers, principals, and guidance counselors, etc.) have skills and expertise in establishing helping relationships, resolving conflicts, solving problems, and mediating issues. Staff development programs in these areas should be provided for the faculty and staff.

The school should also offer similar workshops and classes for the families so they can enhance their skills. These parent education best practices are described in the Coaching Strategy (chapter 10).

The following are some guidelines for the problem-solving parent/teacher conference:

Planning the Conference

As for the Type 1 conference, it is important to arrange the meeting so that it is as easy as possible for the families to participate in the best possible atmosphere. Some of the following suggestions are similar to those listed under the Type 1 conference; however, they have been modified to respond in a helping way specifically to distressed families.

- If you are scheduling the meeting, depending on how urgent the issue or problem is, be flexible on the time and date. To help establish a positive atmosphere, be accommodating and hold the meeting when the parents are most available, such as early in the morning, late in the afternoons, and evenings.

- Be sensitive to language and cultural differences. Make contact in home language and have interpreters available at the conference if the family members do not speak fluent English. If the issue isn't too sensitive, and if the parent agrees, ask a parent volunteer from the neighborhood to act as a translator. This can make the family more comfortable.
- If the family is initiating the meeting, try to gather enough information to ascertain the nature of the issue, problem, or concern so you can be prepared to respond.
- Ask the parents if they will need child care.
- Provide transportation to and from the conference, if no other way is available.
- Consider holding the conference somewhere in the family's neighborhood, usually a community center, an apartment clubhouse, social agency conference room, or similar location. You will have to assess the situation to determine if it would be in the family and the school's best interests to hold the meeting in the home. Having the meeting away from the school is an especially good idea if the family is not well connected and/or is alienated from the school. Meeting in the family's home territory can reduce anxieties and signals to the parents that you want to work with them.
- If the school is scheduling the conference, inform the family of the problem, issue, or concern so the family members can be prepared. Let them know the purpose of the meeting is to solve problems and that you want the conference to be a win-win experience for everyone.
- Consult with all appropriate faculty, staff, and resource personnel to get their perspectives on the problem, issue, or concern. Advise them of the upcoming conference and, if necessary, have them attend the meeting, or be on call. This is especially important if the conference relates to a student with special needs.
- If you think it appropriate, or if conditions warrant, invite or ask the parent to bring the student to the meeting. Whether the child attends or not, both the teacher and parent should discuss the purpose of the conference with him or her before the meeting occurs.
- Before the meeting, if possible, provide the parent with documents and materials related to the issue to be discussed. This includes such things as policies dealing with discipline, grading, the curriculum, and athletic requirements; and copies of student work, exams and projects, referral sheets, absence notes, and progress reports.
- When the parent asks for a conference on short notice, or if the family shows up unannounced at the school with a concern, you may not have time to get the pertinent materials to the parent prior to the meeting. In this

case, gather as many of the documents as possible, and have them available at the meeting. It is important to anticipate meetings of this sort, and to have policy materials handy. The need to document inappropriate student behavior and unsatisfactory progress is obvious.

- If you have time, suggest that the parents prepare questions and gather information related to the issue or concern.
- Organize a folder with examples of the student's work and test results and any notes or questions from the parent.
- Prepare an agenda for the conference. Organize the information that is related to the problem, issue, or concern. Determine what information you need from the parent.
- Prior to the meeting, discuss and review possible solutions, alternatives, and contingencies with other relevant individuals. Determine what is acceptable and what is not. You will have to have this baseline information before you can make decisions and negotiate effectively.
- Identify potential areas to be included in a collaborative action plan to be agreed upon by the family and school.
- Ask the parent to bring any relevant medical information such as allergies; vision, speech, or hearing problems; and so forth.

Conducting the Conference

- Conduct the conference in a respectful and caring way. Concerns, opinions, and suggestions should be shared openly and honestly.
- Choose your words carefully because what you say will have either a positive or a negative impact on the problem-solving dynamics of the conference.
- Don't talk education jargon. Let the parents know it is appropriate to ask you to explain any terms or concepts that they do not understand.
- Hold the meeting in a conference room or office so there will be privacy so the discussion won't be overheard.
- Have chairs available for all family members and staff who may be present. It is awkward to have to excuse yourself to locate more chairs after the family has arrived. Offering the family coffee, tea, or a soft drink can help set a positive tone and reduce negative feelings.
- If you have called the meeting, describe the problem, issue, or concern with the parents. Let them know, again, that you want the meeting to be a win-win experience for everyone. Encourage the parents to take notes.
- If appropriate, review the child's strengths and weaknesses, beginning with the strengths. Ask the parents to share their perception of the child's strengths and weaknesses based on their observations.

- Assure the parents that their knowledge of their child is an important part of assessing the problem. A more complete picture of the child's needs and strengths can be obtained by combining their information with the information that you have gathered or observed yourself.
- Describe how what you are seeing in the child's behavior and attitude represents his or her progress. For example, describe how the child is missing out on learning opportunities. Do not dwell on how you, or the other children, are affected.
- Review with the parent what you have tried so far and share the results. Ask the parents if they have any questions, comments, or suggestions.
- If the parents requested the conference, ask them to describe the problem, issue, or concern. Listen carefully and ask the parent if you can take notes. After the parent has finished with the description, ask questions for clarification or additional information.
- Empathize with the family and inform them that you want to be helpful. Acknowledge that the family's feelings are real and normal.
- Inform the family that you consider the conference to be a meeting between equal partners. Be very sensitive not to patronize or demean the parent or child.
- When the conference is called to make an assessment or develop a program for a child with special needs, be prepared to with developmental information about the child. Explain to parents why and how early identification and intervention are beneficial.

  Have referral information that describes the law and process and gives names and telephone numbers. Offer to be part of the process to whatever degree they want you to be involved. Remind them that they are in charge. They have the final say about what is right for their child.
- Attempt to identify solutions or alternatives to resolve the issue, problem, or concern. If appropriate, develop a plan of action and reach a consensus on any steps that need to be taken to enhance the child's academic and social development both at home and at school.
- Identify ways you and the parent will work together to implement the plan.
- If appropriate, initiate a learning contract between the child, parent, and teacher that outlines responsibilities and goals for all parties.
- End the conference by summarizing the child's strengths, areas for growth, and the action plan. Discuss follow-up procedures.

Follow-up to the Conference

- Follow through with any collaborative action plan agreed upon in the conference.

- Send a letter describing the outcome of the meeting and the action taken. Emphasize to the parents how important it is to you and the child to have a good working relationship between family and school. Ask if they have any questions or need more information.
- If a problem-solving action plan has been initiated between the school and the family, follow-up with a phone call in two to four weeks. Inform the family about progress on your end, and check on the family's progress. If necessary, plan the next step.
- If the child did not attend the conference, establish a time when the teacher and parent can review the outcome of the conference with the child.
- Share outcomes of the meeting with other school personnel if needed.
- Evaluate the conference and action plan to determine if the issue, problem, or concern was resolved in a satisfactory way.

Communicating When Things Are Not Going So Good

In his book, The Road Less Traveled, *M. Scott Peck argues that once we accept one of the greatest truths, which is that "life is difficult," then things become easier. I believe he means that because there will be problems, we need to learn to be good problem-solvers. Our lives will be less difficult if we are good problem-solvers. Teachers, principals, counselors, and parents have the responsibility to be good at solving problems for themselves, and also for the children. It is a function of the school and the family to respond to children when they are having difficulties and to help them learn to be good problem-solvers. Therefore, the school and families need to be able to communicate effectively when problems arise.*

If it is observed that a child is experiencing difficulties or has shown a dramatic change in behavior, it is essential that someone close to the student contacts the family immediately. The school must use a collaborative approach when communicating with the family. By working together, the school and family will have a better chance of solving the problem. It is important that the child knows that the family and school are partners as otherwise he or she might try to work the parent against the school and vice versa. Many times the family wants help but is afraid or embarrassed to ask. In other cases, parents are not aware of a problem.

Group Communicating: Meetings, Events, and Activities

Collaboration is the common thread running throughout all of the best practices. Development of the partnerships should be a goal when organizing, scheduling, and hosting meetings, events, and activities for the families. Some guidelines for reaching out to the parents and increasing and maintaining participation at such events as open houses, PTA meetings, parent education sessions, social events, and other activities are:

- Be flexible when organizing meetings, events, and activities. Try to adjust the dates and times to fit the schedules of the families. Be aware of church or club regular meeting times, work shifts, and so forth, when scheduling meetings.
- Provide free transportation and child care. Some schools use their activity bus to transport the parents to and from school. Parents, teachers, and students are usually willing to volunteer to supervise activity centers for the children or take care of babies. This can be a project for the high school's early childhood class. Have fun learning activities available to entertain the children during the meeting.
- Conduct bilingual PTA/PTO meetings, if appropriate. Send notices in parents' native language. Have translators and sign language interpreters available for non-English-speaking and hearing-impaired family members when appropriate. Enlist school representatives or recruit community volunteers who are fluent in the language of ethnic groups.
- Begin the meetings on a positive note. This will set the tone for the rest of the activity.
- At business meetings, gather parent ideas. The families need to feel that they are heard. The school should act as an incubator of ideas and be a place where change and innovations are supported.
- To get parents acquainted at a PTA/PTO meeting, ask them to break into groups that correspond to their children's grade levels. The parents tell the other members of the group about their children and themselves.
- Have students write letters to their parents inviting them to attend the events.
- Stamp a picture of the school's mascot or a smiling face on the child's hand to remind the family of an evening meeting, or make a string necklace with a picture of an animal and a meeting notice. These gentle reminders are helpful.
- Ask PTA/PTO members to call and invite family members to attend and arrange for transportation if necessary. They meet and host the parents at the meeting and introduce the parents to other members. You can use a telephone tree to organize the calls.
- Recognize participation with thank-you notes, special tags and ribbons, and similar gestures. Gold stars can be placed on family members' name tags as an award for attendance, service, and so on. Awards and recognition are very special to all parents, and the stars are very important to them.

- Take pictures of important and interesting events where students and/or family members are involved. Make double prints to send pictures to the families.
- You can also videotape the parent involvement events. The tapes can be shown at PTA and other family meetings, open houses, and so on. Some schools have created a "tape library" so the families can borrow or copy tapes.

Classroom orientations. Schedule a convenient time for the families to come to an orientation meeting to learn about the organization of the children's classrooms and the teacher's philosophy, rules, and procedures. The format should be an open discussion between the parents and teachers. It is a good idea for the teachers to post their philosophy outside their classroom door for all to see.

User-Friendly Room Location
If parents are not familiar with the school, have the meetings in a room located close to the parking lot and the entrance to the building. Have lots of lights on in the room and halls. Not only will this help the families find the room, but also arriving parents will be more comfortable when they can see other parents and teachers in the room from the parking lot.

Muffins with moms and doughnuts with dads. Schedule early-morning or late-afternoon informal meeting times with parents. Organize the meetings around light refreshments. No appointments or reservations are necessary and there is no agenda. The time is used for getting acquainted, asking questions, obtaining information, and discussing issues. Catchy titles add to the informal nature of the meetings.

Lunch with your child. Invite the parents to come and have lunch or breakfast with their child. Ask the parents to let you know in advance so arrangements can be made. For the parents to come to school and eat with their children demonstrates they are in partnership with the teachers.

Informal group luncheons. Invite the families to school to have lunch at school. The luncheons provide an opportunity for parents, grandparents, and other family members to interact with the faculty and staff and with each other.

These luncheons work well for parents of middle- and high-school students. Usually, these students are not comfortable having their families coming to school to eat lunch with them, but they like to see their parents in school. It is an event that shows the students that the parents are involved.

Grandparents' day. Grandparents are invited to school to eat lunch or breakfast with their grandchildren. Before or after the meal, grandparents can visit the classrooms and tell stories about their childhood, culture, family life, and vocation to the whole class.

The Open House

The open house is a common group communicating activity. Traditionally, the event has multiple purposes that include bringing the families into the school and providing them with the opportunity to learn about the school program, increasing PTA/PTO membership, and acquainting families with the faculty and staff. Most schools have open houses and the event is a mainstay of many parent involvement programs. Often open houses are well attended, especially in the elementary schools, and usually families are satisfied with the activity.

However, even with the more successful open houses, there usually is a segment of the family population that is missing. And, sometimes those parents who do show up do not feel they got what they came for. Therefore, it is important to evaluate our open house procedures to see if they doing all that we would like them to do. At times, we continue with a program in a certain way because it is the way it has always been done, and no one has questioned if it is meeting the objectives. It is quite possible the event could be improved with some refinements and adjustments.

Traditional formats. Let us consider what the typical open house looks like. We have all experienced them. Open houses are usually scheduled early in the school year and are held on a week night. The event begins with the first business meeting of the PTA/PTO in the school's cafeteria. The benefits of the organization are hyped, the various fund-raising activities are described, officers are introduced, and membership is sought. Then the principal talks to the families about the school's programs, activities, discipline, and other policies. He or she emphasizes the importance of the parents being involvement and expresses the hope that they will be available to act as volunteers.

This is the preamble to the actual open house. The families sit politely and patiently, trying to keep their kids quiet and waiting for the real show to start. Finally, someone tells the parents how the open house will be run. Usually, they already know. The rules and procedures are described in detail, and it is announced that at the end of the open house the families are invited back to the cafeteria for refreshments.

In elementary schools, the parents are directed to the child's classroom to meet with the teacher. The teacher talks with the families as a group and informs them about the curriculum, classroom management, rules, and procedures, and his or her availability to meet with the parents. During the discussion, the teacher may ask the family members to serve as volunteers, chaperones, and classroom moms and/or dads.

In middle schools and high schools, the parents are instructed to follow an abbreviated form of their child's class schedule. Because there is such a limited time allotted for each class period, the parents are asked not to ask the teacher questions or try to get information about their child. The families then go to the first period class to meet with the teacher for a brief meeting. The teacher quickly informs the family about the nature of the course and how he or she will manage the class. After a few minutes, the bell rings again and the family moves on to the next class. This process is repeated until the family has moved through their child's entire schedule. After the last period, the parents return to the cafeteria for cookies and punch.

Doesn't this sound familiar? I've been to many open houses as a parent, teacher, and principal. At the high school my kids attended, there was usually a good turnout of parents. Now as I think about it, those who attended were mostly the middle-class core that also attended the band concerts, football games, and other activities.

However, I also recall that when I was a principal at a high school in a middle- to lower-class rural school district there were more teachers present at the open houses than parents. The elementary school was located on the same campus and parents generally turned out for their open houses and not ours. At the time the low attendance did not trouble me too much. I thought it was just the way it was. Now, I realize that we should have made an effort to reach the missing parents.

ADJUSTMENTS AND REFINEMENTS

I do not want to leave the impression that I think the traditional way open houses are conducted is all bad. However, I do believe adjustments and refinements can be made to make them better and to reach more parents.

Self-Interests

As we consider making changes, it is important to identify the typical self-interests of the different parties. The school is interested in informing the parents about the curriculum and programs and would like to have the support of the families. The PTA/PTO would also like the support of the families and increase their membership.

Within this context, the parents' primary self-interest is their child. They would like to know about the curriculum, programs, and activities and their child's teacher. The families will want to find out how they can help their child have a successful year. In many cases, the parents are frustrated if they do not have the opportunity to discuss their child's needs with the teacher.

Consequently, it is usually hard to meet the self-interests of the various parties at one open house. If building partnerships with the families is going to be a major focus, rather than opening the year with the usual open house and PTO/PTA business meeting, host a family picnic instead. The families bring part of the meal and the school supplies the rest. When the family population is not very connected, the school can provide the food (see the family picnic best practice in the Connecting chapter).

The picnic is an opportunity to welcome the families to the learning community and for people to get acquainted. Students, acting as best buddies or school ambassadors, give the parents and new student tours of the school. The school band and chorus can perform. Transportation is provided to parents if needed. The school and the PTA can set up places where the families can get information and ask questions.

To meet other self-interests, a more typical open house can be scheduled after school opens. The teachers can meet with parents as a group and the PTA can have a business meeting. At the open house, the teachers can let the parents know when they are available to meet with them individually to discuss their child. The school can schedule certain evenings and even weekend days for the parents to meet with the teachers. Some schools schedule different open house for each grade level. This helps parents with more than one child at the school. If possible, the faculty members need to be compensated for the extra time spent at school. By organizing and scheduling events and activities to meet the self-interests of the different shareholders, partnerships can be formed and strengthened.

Mass Communicating

Sometimes, mass communication best practices are very effective in informing the families and community about the school and partnership activities. Different best practices can be used to display the family and school's commitment to quality education and the importance of working together. The following are some mass communicating best practices.

Letter campaigns. Letters and flyers from the clergy, civic clubs, chamber of commerce, company publications, hospitals, banks, grocery stores, and so on, can be sent to the students' homes. The letters urge the families to get involved at home and school, attend meetings and workshops, and support the school and its programs.

Bumper stickers. Provide bumper stickers for parents and community members that send positive messages about the child and the school. Examples of child-directed stickers include:

- I Have a Super Kid at Fort Mill Middle School.
- My Child Has Read 100 Books.

- I Am a Parent of a Terrific Student at Central High.
- I Have Great Kids.

A school-directed bumper sticker is also a way to communicate the school's collective vision and positive slogan. This is an inexpensive way to spread the word throughout the school and neighborhoods and to build commitment. Some examples of messages on stickers are:

- On the Move with Morris High
- Catch the Olympic Pride
- Excellence at Eastover Elementary
- Caring and Sharing at Berryhill

Reactionary Bumper Stickers
There is one bumper sticker that I have mixed feelings about. It is the one that states, "I have an honor student at . . . School."

I desire excellence, but I also covet equity. Excellence without equity is limited. Only a few students are recognized as honor students. These stickers do recognize the child, but do little to build the learning community. There are many kids who are successful and hardworking, but are not selected as "honor" students. These children and families need to be recognized as well.

This elitism is vented in a reactionary sticker that I have seen that says, "My kid just beat up your honor student." Even though it can be argued that the sticker is supposed to be funny, it sends a serious message. The honor student sticker isolates some families from the school.

T-shirts. Have colorful T-shirts made with a picture of the school mascot or logo and an involvement slogan such as: We are good, but we can be better; Education is a family affair; Working together for excellence; and so on. Some schools print their mission statements on the shirts.

The T-shirts are sold by the PTA/PTO, School Improvement Council, and other organizations, and they are excellent appreciation and recognition gifts.

Billboards. Rent billboards to promote such events as parent-teacher conferences, open houses, career fairs, test administration dates, and school awards. One North Carolina school district rents a billboard along the main road on a regular basis, and I always look for it when I drive across the state. The companies that rent the billboards are usually willing to give the schools a reduced price. Also, organizations such as the PTA/PTO, service clubs, and business can be approached to help defer the cost.

Theater marquees. Contact local theater managers to see if you can post special messages to the families along with the movie titles. Only ask to use them for important meetings and events (e.g., open house, parent-teacher conferences, standardized test dates, graduation, etc.).

Electric school marquees. Many schools have electric marquees that advertise and promote school and partnership activities and events. Raising money to purchase a marquees is a good PTA, parent group, or class project.

Student exhibits. A rotating display of projects in many disciplines such as art, science, social studies, industrial arts, and human ecology is a positive educational message to families and other visitors. Besides the school, airports, hospitals, government buildings, education centers, and performance halls are excellent sites for such displays. The exhibits are a chance to show the many talents of the students and are great for public relations.

Notify the parents when and where their child's work is being exhibited and invite them to see the display. Take photographs of the parents and their students next to the display. Include the photographs as part of the exhibit. Give copies of the pictures to the families and also send them to local newspapers.

Omaha's Creative Billboards

Back in the 1990s, the Omaha Public Schools had a wonderful Youth Art Month program where student art is displayed on over 50 outdoor billboards throughout the city. In March, with the cooperation of local businesses and agencies and the Imperial Sign Company, student art work was chosen to be reproduced by the sign company's artists and displayed on billboards. On each billboard, the name of the student's sponsor and the school's name was listed along with the student's work. The original pieces of art were displayed at a reception for the student artist, parents, principals, teachers, and sponsors.

I was told of one case where the student and her mother did not have transportation so the school took them to the site where her work was on a billboard. The mother and daughter couldn't believe what they saw and they stood spellbound for several minutes. It was an experience that they will never forget.

Currently, the student art month is celebrated with a wonderful slide presentation on the district's website. This is impressive, but the billboards had city-wide impact.

Door-to-door flyers. When organizing such things as partnership and school improvement programs, new family services, building programs, and so forth, parents, students, and community members volunteer to distribute publicity and informational flyers through the neighborhoods. The material is left in newspaper and mail boxes, on door knobs, and in other convenient locations.

Drive-in windows. Notices about meetings, workshops, parent-teacher conferences, and standardized test dates can be displayed and distributed at bank and fast-food drive-in windows.

Newspapers. Publicize partnership and school programs through the daily newspapers. In addition to sending them materials, notify the papers in advance so they can send a reporter to cover the events and activities. Many papers have a family section and a neighborhood news insert. Don't forget the local weekly newspapers. These publications are eager for local school and neighborhood news and they will use photographs.

District and school websites. Most districts and schools have their own websites. There is virtually no limit to kinds of information that can be posted on these sites. However, as noted earlier, be aware that many hard-to-reach parents do not have access to computers and may not be comfortable using the computer, even if one is available. However, the children will often know how to use the computer even if the parent doesn't.

Local businesses, companies, and industries. Identify businesses and industries where many of the parents work, and ask employers if they are willing to help. Information materials, announcements, and invitations can be placed in their newsletters, on bulletin boards, in paycheck envelopes, and so forth. Businesses are usually willing to place posters and bulletins in their store windows as well.

Many organizations are willing to host parent meetings and other activities. Some companies are even willing to establish family rooms with parenting materials in their facilities.

Utility bills. Natural gas, electric, telephone, television cable service companies, and similar organizations are often willing to include educational and partnership information, announcements, and invitations in their regular billing envelopes. Messages can be printed on the envelopes themselves.

Shopping bags. Information about the importance of parent involvement and being partners with the school is printed on grocery and department store plastic and paper bags.

Church bulletins. Contact the clergy in the families' neighborhoods and ask if information about partnerships events and activities can be placed their newsletter to members.

Poster contests. Conduct poster contests to publicize open houses, family picnics, and other events. Place the posters in stores and shops around the community. Don't make the contest a big competition thing, but a win-win activity: Everyone is a winner and there are lots of small prizes.

COORDINATING: BUILDING ON THE CONNECTING AND COMMUNICATING STRATEGIES

The next chapter presents best practices that can be used to coordinate service and resources to needy families. Programs and activities for supporting the school are also included in this chapter.

Chapter 8

Coordinating: Getting It Together

Table 8.1

Connecting	Communicating	Coordinating	Coaching

As stated in chapter 3, the underlying notion of the family/school partnership concept is that everyone is a stakeholder in the education of children. It is essential that social agencies, businesses, industries, colleges, universities, churches, synagogues, hospitals, service clubs, and community members work with the families and schools to enhance the academic and social development of the children. However, as mentioned before, this kind of collaboration is not the norm.

Sometimes children's educational and social development needs are pushed into the background as the parents attempt to deal with major problems and concerns such as lack of food, clothing, transportation, housing, health care, unemployment, a child with special needs, drug and alcohol abuse, and teenage pregnancy. The Coordinating Strategy is intended to help resolve some of these issues by intervening with programs and activities.

For a variety of reasons, many families are not receiving the services and resources from the community and school that would help improve their lives and involve them in the education of their children. Therefore, the Coordinating Collaboration Strategy is designed to:

- increase family awareness of availability of school and community services and resources
- ensure that school and community services and resources are accessible to all families in need
- facilitate the creation of new family services and resources

The assumption is by improving the conditions at home and taking care of immediate family needs, the parents will have a greater capacity to be involved with their children's education. This strategy builds on the collaborative relationships formed by the Connecting and Communicating Strategies.

The next section describes different types of programs and activities where the school and community, especially the social agencies, work together to coordinate and provide services and resources to overburdened families.

COORDINATING SERVICES AND RESOURCES

Using the Coordinating Strategy, programs can be implemented where the school and community combine and "broker" services and resources. There are at least four major reasons why services and resources are not reaching families in need. First, the services and resources are not available in the community. Second, families are not aware of existing services and resources. Third, they do not know how to go about obtaining the services and resources. And fourth, social and governmental agencies are very complex and fragmented, and interagency cooperation is not common.

The Coordinating Strategy requires that all parties move beyond their organizational walls and work for the common good of children. Coordinating services and resources can be tricky because it involves combining the educational, business, and social service models. The bottom line is that often several organizations are targeting the same populations with intervention strategies designed to reach similar goals and by combining forces, some of the governmental fragmentation can be eliminated.

COORDINATING BEST PRACTICES

The following programs, events, and activities are organized so that the least labor-intensive appear first, followed by those that are more comprehensive. For example, some best practices for helping the families are as simple as publishing directories listing and describing available services and resources. Other programs are quite complex. For instance, a comprehensive intra-agency school-based center is described where a variety of services are rendered to the families at one location in the neighborhood.

It is crucial that various stakeholders (parents, teachers, principals, community leaders) know and understand what services and resources are available and how to access them. Developing this understanding reaps large dividends and does not require a great deal of money or personnel to accomplish. The following are some best practices to accomplish this.

Services and Resources Directory

Develop and publish a directory of social and community service agencies that includes a description of programs, addresses, telephone numbers, and names of representatives to be contacted. The directory lists social service agencies, crisis centers, health clinics, service clubs, and school resource centers. In addition, it includes such facilities as food pantries, clothing centers, reading and language centers, museums, nature centers, and libraries.

Electronic Directories

Place the directory of services and resources on the school's website so that it is easily accessible to school and community personnel. List e-mail addresses, telephone, and fax numbers so school and community personnel can network with each other. An electronic newsletter can be sent out to keep users informed about changes, new programs, and ideas.

Family Forums

Schedule informational family meetings on such topics as Social Security benefits, Aid for Dependent Children (AFDC), food stamps, how to get electric power service restored, available health services, and how to obtain domestic violence help and counseling. At the meetings, family members meet school and social service representatives, and are able to ask questions about programs and procedures.

If the parents are not very connected with the school, or if the school is located a distance from the families, it is a good idea to hold the forums in the neighborhoods; for example, in churches, synagogues, community centers, or business or hospital conference rooms.

Service and Resource Referral Committee

A group of parent and community volunteers are organized to be an informational and referral service for families who need child care, after-school and weekend recreation programs, cultural events, transportation to the library, and other social services.

School/Community Coordinating Committee

A committee made up of teachers, administrators, guidance counselors, social workers, and parents is established to help coordinate services and resources to needy families. If the school is fortunate enough to have a family/school coordinator, that person can chair the committee. The committee is notified when a teacher, principal, counselor, parent, or coordinator discovers a family facing a problem that is preventing the family members from effectively playing their parenting roles.

I witnessed a successful committee action at one school in Nashville. A teacher looked out of the window and saw a mother beating her two young children with a stick. The teacher got the principal, and they stopped the woman and took the stick away. It was obvious that the mother was spaced out on drugs. They took the woman and the children to the office and telephoned the school's social worker.

The family/school coordinator was called to the office and an impromptu community/school coordinating committee meeting was held when the social worker arrived. Because they were prepared, the Department of Social Services was able to care for the woman's two children, and the mother was taken to the hospital.

The next day, the mother was admitted to a drug rehabilitation program and the children placed in foster care. The mother had been participating in a parent education program at school. When she was released from the rehabilitation center, she continued coming to the parent club meetings, even after the children were taken from her.

This is a real success story, because eventually the mother was in recovery, and the children were returned to her. Her involvement with the school expanded. In fact, eventually she was hired to be one of the teachers for the parent club's literacy program. Without the swift action by the school/community coordinating committee, both the children and the mother would probably have been lost.

Family Resource Centers

An array of facilities could be categorized as "family resource centers." These are places where family members can go for information, training, support, resources, services, and even food, clothing, and shelter. The centers have such titles as family rooms, family resource centers, family service centers, and family food pantries, and clothing centers.

Usually, the centers are located in or near the school, but sometimes they are housed in the neighborhoods or at a central location away from the school. These locations may be more convenient to get to and can help make connections with the families. This is particularly important for those family populations who are not comfortable in a school setting. Located away from the school and in the neighborhood, the center is perceived as inviting and accessible.

Parent or family rooms. While the primary function of this kind of center is to connect and communicate with the families, family rooms are excellent settings for providing information and instruction about services and resources.

The family rooms usually have information available on such things as: parenting, drug abuse, nutrition, school curriculum and policies, and other relevant subjects.

The ideal family center will have books, audiotapes and videotapes, games, puzzles, telephones, computers, copying machines, software, and so forth. Adequate space will also be available for classes, workshops, support groups, and child care.

Some centers even have kitchens, laundry rooms, and sewing machines to help the families. In brief, the facilities should reflect the needs of the targeted families.

Family centers should be user-friendly and look, feel, and smell like a welcoming environment. This is especially important for those families that do not live in comfortable conditions. For example, have fresh flowers in the center, and if facilities are available, occasionally have cookies baking or other foods cooking to create a nice ambience. The centers should be places the parents look forward to visiting.

A Cooperative Learning Center

In Buffalo, New York, the school district, in cooperation with the Urban League operates a family center in the downtown area. This center began in 1989: a first in the state. Housed in a marvelous building that formerly served as a bank, the center includes an Even Start program with preschool and nursery facilities. School buses are used to transport the parents to the center and for field trips. Parents enroll in a variety of classes and workshops dealing with life skills, parenting, foreign languages, GED preparation, and general education. There is also a computer lab with an extensive network of software. The center is a fine example of cooperation between the city schools and the private sector. Seeing the preschool children and teachers working together in the room that contains the large bank vault is a reminder of the collaborative relationship between the schools and the private sector.

Cycling out Parent Supervisor

In Omaha, Nebraska, the school district hires parents to supervise the family rooms in the schools. The parents are paid at the minimum wage rate and the district provides them with free in-service job training when they are not on duty. The goal of the training is for the parents to be able to break out of the poverty cycle and get better higher paying jobs in the school or community. When the family room supervisors "cycle out" to different jobs, new parents are hired and the process is repeated.

Food pantries and clothing centers. Food pantries and clothing centers are established so families in need can obtain emergency supplies. These are located in the school, neighborhoods, or a central location. In schools, they can be located near the parent room, family resource center, main office, or in a spare room or trailer. In the neighborhoods, centers and pantries can be housed in community centers, churches, synagogues, and so on. Some school districts have one central location (e.g., the staff development center, warehouses, etc.). Obviously, the centers and pantries need to be located where they are easily accessible and where families are comfortable going.

School-based family resource centers. The primary function of this type of center is to link needy families to services and resources in the community. The goal is to enhance the students' abilities to succeed in school by helping children and their families to solve problems and meet their basic needs.

The center directors, who are often teachers, work closely with the school faculty to assess needs and to coordinate the services. The director and his or her staff members serve as advocates for the families. In this type of center, the social service agencies collaborate with the center staff, but services are not based at the center. The director builds a rich network of agencies that can be called on when needed.

The following is an example of how well a family resource center can work. When I was visiting a center in Kentucky, the director related to me how she was able to respond to a family in crisis. One morning when she arrived at the center, which is located in a portable classroom outside an elementary school, she found a mother and her two children sitting in a car. The mother was waiting for her and had come to get help. The night before, her husband had beaten her and threatened to kill her and the children. She was afraid and did not know what to do.

The director contacted a women's center, the police, the domestic violence court, and a social worker. During that day, she was able to place the woman and the children in a shelter, had an injunction order issued against the husband, obtained financial assistance, and arranged for a police escort to protect the woman so she could retrieve some belongings from the house. This coordinated response would never have happened without the network the director had established with the various agencies in the community.

Hawaii Healthy Start Program

Hawaii's Healthy Start Program is built on the premise that certain families because of single parenthood, poverty, lack of education or support, need help to build positive parenting skills and promote healthy development of their children. In 1995, the Hawaii legislature appropriated $6 million for the program.

Healthy Start workers screen the records of half of the 18,000 babies born in Hawaii each year. The screenings look for risk factors such as domestic violence, lack of prenatal care, attempted abortions, and signs of substance abuse. The parents are contacted and weekly home visits are made by para-professionals who are high-school graduates from the same communities as the parents. The home visitors work with the parents to enhance their nurturing and teacher roles.

School-based limited-service family centers. Some centers have a few agency representatives located at the school site that collaborate with the center director and school faculty and staff. Social workers, Communities-in-Schools counselors, youth agency representatives, and others have offices in the school where they can meet with the students and families. These "outside" people become an integral part of the faculty and staff. They can respond quickly when problems arise and needs are identified.

I visited a family resource center located in a California middle school that had agency representatives assigned to the school. Juvenile court representatives, county attendance officers, Communities-in-Schools, and other social agency representatives were assigned to the school to counsel and advise the students and families. The center director reached out and worked with the families to get them involved, and coordinated the services and resources.

In addition to her other responsibilities, the director supervised the school's in-house suspension program. Most of the students sent to her for disciplinary reasons were prime candidates for the agency representatives. By coordinating their programs, the school and agencies were able to help many of the adolescents before they failed in school, dropped out, or got into real trouble.

School-Based Full-Service Family Centers

At this type of center, families can obtain services and resources on site. The families can do one-stop shopping. An example of a very comprehensive intra-agency school-based center is located in Louisville, Kentucky. This collaborative endeavor, called The Neighborhood Place, was established in conjunction with the school and county to deliver services to the parents and children in a lower socioeconomic community. The nationally recognized center began in 1993 and serves as a main access point in the service delivery system by identifying, coordinating, and rendering existing services. If services are not available on site, the center serves as the catalyst for the development of such resources. Core services available at the Neighborhood Place include:

- health services that include school physical examinations, immunizations, health education, and other services

- child care that includes infant and toddler care, part-time before- and after-school care, summertime care, and a Parents' Day Out program, which is coordinated with the local churches, synagogues, and other community agencies
- a "families in training" program that includes parent support groups, nutrition education, family empowerment sessions, behavioral problem programs, and literacy classes for parents
- mental health, and drug and alcohol abuse counseling that includes assessment and evaluation, individual therapy, group sessions, recovery groups, and access to specialized child and family services, such as acute psychiatric and domestic violence care
- family financial assistance programs that include food stamps, aid to financially dependent children, subsidized daycare, and emergency financial assistance
- employment services that offer counseling, job training, mentoring, preemployment skill development, and part-time employment

The Neighborhood Places are funded by the Louisville/Jefferson County government and the school system. (There are now eight.) This type of center is very effective and cost efficient.

An example of how well this interagency approach works is illustrated by the way the center deals with the immunization. Before any child can attend school, the parent must provide evidence that the child has been immunized for different diseases. If the parent fails to do so, the matter is turned over to the courts, because the child is not attending school. As you can imagine, the time and money involved in all the referrals and court costs is enormous.

At the Neighborhood Place, the child can be examined and immunized at school before enrolling. The child and families are screened for other problems, and if any are identified, social service and school representatives are available at the center to provide counseling and resources. Because of the Neighborhood Place, the problem of children arriving at school without their shots has virtually been eliminated in this community.

COACHING: BUILDING ON THE OTHER PARTNERSHIP INTERVENTION STRATEGIES

The Coaching Strategy is presented in the next chapter. This intervention builds on the first three Partnership Intervention Strategies. While the first strategies are primarily concerned with overcoming barriers, establishing communication flows, and coordinating services, the Coaching Strategy is designed to enhance the families' ability to play their parenting roles. By using the Connecting, Communicating, and Coordinating strategies to build collaborative relationships with the families, the school is in the position to help the parents learn how to get involved in the social and academic development of their children. The Coaching Strategy used in conjunction with the other interventions will help solve "the case of the missing families."

Chapter 9

Coaching: Building a Team

Table 9.1

Connecting	Communicating	Coordinating	Coaching

A good friend of mine, Suzanne Brown, told me a wonderful story that captures the spirit of the Coaching Strategy. Suzanne was a family/school coordinator and director of a parent involvement program at an inner-city elementary school in Nashville. One day, when she was out in the neighborhood visiting families, one of her parents approached from the other side of the street.

Suzanne waved to the woman as she drew closer. The woman waved back and shouted across the street, "You gotta reach the parents to reach the kids." This remark was insightful and profound. Paraphrasing the mother's statement, the function of the Coaching Strategy is to "reach and empower the parents so they can reach their kids."

Parenting is often an overwhelming task, particularly for families who do not have the appropriate skills and knowledge. The Coaching Strategy is used to help the parents to enhance their capacities to play the eight Parent Partner Roles. The notion of enhancing family members' capacities to play their roles is a subtle, but crucial way of thinking about the process.

As discussed in chapter 5, the Partnership Intervention Strategies are progressive and hierarchical. Coaching is the most progressive strategy and builds on the collaborative relationships formed by the Connecting, Communicating, and Coordinating Intervention strategies.

Certainly, the intent of the strategy is for the parents to acquire new skills and knowledge, but coaching is an act of mentoring to achieve the goals. It has been said that "a coach guides from the side, rather than being a sage on the stage." The coach does not give you the answers, but leads you toward the solution.

Therefore, the Coaching Strategy is designed to:

- enhance the parents' ability and capacity to effectively play the Parent Partner Roles
- enhance the parents' general sense of well-being, knowledge, and skill level

When developing a coaching intervention plan, first identify the parent partner role(s) to be enhanced and then choose a best practice(s) that best fits the situation.

COACHING VENUES AND PARENT SUPPORT

Family centers. Family centers vary in size, ranging from parent corners in classrooms and rooms in the schools or community centers, to separate buildings. Likewise, the programs and services offered by the family centers vary; some are limited in scope, while others are very comprehensive. Many centers start small and then expand as resources and expertise become available. The Coordinating Strategy chapter (chapter 8) presents an in-depth discussion of family resource centers.

Coaching home visits. As discussed in chapter 6, home visits are excellent ways to make connections and establish communication flows with parents. The visits also offer excellent opportunities for coaching.

For example, the home visitors work with the parents to enhance their Parent Partner Role skills and knowledge by modeling behavior and demonstrating home-learning activities with their children. The parents are provided with materials (e.g., books, toys, games, paper, crayons, paints, etc.).

Parent clubs. At the beginning of this chapter, I alluded to what a parent told my friend, Suzanne Brown about working with hard-to-reach parents. Suzanne was a family/school coordinator at an inner-city elementary school in Nashville, Tennessee.

When she started working at the school, there was zero parent involvement. The parents lived in a housing project that surrounded the school. This was a high-crime and drug-trafficking area and many parents were afraid to leave their homes. The parents were generally alienated from the school. Suzanne began making connections by visiting the parents at their homes. You can imagine how surprised the families were to have someone from the school to come to visit and not bring bad news.

Suzanne invited them to come to school the following Monday for a meeting to start a parent club. She described a little about what she had in mind and told them that refreshments would be served. When Monday arrived she asked the school's custodian to set up some chairs in the auditorium/ gymnasium for the meeting. When she went back to check, he had set out about six chairs. He had worked at the school a long time, and he had low expectations as to how many parents would show up.

Over thirty-five parents came to the meeting. Suzanne was thrilled, and the custodian was amazed. The home visits had worked and some initial connections had been made. Suzanne told the parents that a family center had been established in one of the empty classrooms and this would be a place for them to come to learn how to help their children.

The parent club met three mornings a week. Each meeting began with a mantra that exclaimed that they were important, the children were important, and everyone could be successful. The parents were involved in preparing materials to use with their children at home. A lot of the activities involved cutting, pasting, and coloring. Many of the parents never had the opportunity or materials to do these things when they were growing up and now they didn't have them for their children.

The parents had the opportunity to go with the children on field trips to the museum, fire station, library, post office, and such. Many of the parents had never been to many of these places. Suzanne set up appointments for the parents to go to a local high school's cosmetology class to have their hair and nails done. This helped the parents and students.

As the relationships between the school and parents grew stronger, Suzanne began more coaching activities. Setting up reading classes for the parents was an important one. Eventually, she made arrangements for some of the parents to attend a GED class. The family center and parent club became a very important vehicle to help the parents help themselves and their children.

As time went on, the parents were involved in such things as a survival-for-women program, computer classes, and they even put on a play for the students. Suzanne coordinated social services for the parents in need. She set up trips to the local food bank and clothing center. The parents would volunteer in the school as part of their responsibilities.

This is a wonderful example of how this best practice, a parent club, along with the home visits, created a center for connecting, coordinating and coaching. It also served as a safe haven for the parents when crises arose.

Dad's Coloring Moment

One day I was visiting my friend, Sujette Overstreet, at an inner-city elementary school in Nashville. She was the family/school coordinator. (This was not the school where Suzanne Brown was the coordinator.)

Sujette had established a parent club and the parents (all women) were coloring some pictures for their children. After the pictures were finished, the parents would take the pictures to their children's classrooms as a present and to visit the classroom. This was a way to acknowledge the parent's presence to the child and get them involved in the classroom.

As the parents were working along, two men knocked at the open door. Sujette asked if she could help them. The men said they were there to deliver lunch bags to their children and they didn't know where the classrooms were. After Sujette gave them directions, one of the men asked what the women were doing. After she explained, she asked them if they would like to color a picture for their child. I thought, no way, but they said that they would like to. Sujette being clever and wise had immediately seen an opportunity to provide a connecting and teachable moment with the dads.

The two men colored and worked on their pictures for over 30 minutes. After completing the pictures, they took the lunches and pictures to their children.

First, I was surprised that they would color the pictures. Then, I realized, these dads, like the moms, really enjoyed the opportunity. It is likely that they did not have many of experiences with coloring, cutting, and pasting, or other similar projects.

Workshops and classes. Offering parent education workshops and classes is a popular and efficient way to enhance family members' ability and capacity to assume the eight Parent Partner Roles. Some of the workshops and classes focus directly on educational, social, and parenting issues, while others have a broader focus, designed to enhance the family's overall condition and general sense of well-being.

The more general high-interest sessions are helpful in reaching those families that are not very connected. Offering classes and workshops on such topics as craft-making, cooking, hobbies, car repair, and so on, will attract parents to the school. After the parents are involved, they can be encouraged to take other classes that deal directly with the Parent Partner Roles.

The workshops that focus on ways to improve quality of life have a broad appeal not only to families, but also to some faculty and staff as well. An added benefit is that when parents and teachers participate together in the sessions, collaborative relationships are built and connections between the families and the school are strengthened.

Suggested topics for workshops and classes are presented in the sections related to each of the Parent Partner Roles.

Why Angels Can Fly

A Scottish proverb says, *"The reason angels can fly is that they take themselves so lightly."* While education is serious business, it should be enjoyable *as well. The workshops and classes should be as positive and upbeat as possible. Always try to include activities that are fun. Suggestions for making the parent education programs fun and enjoyable are included in this chapter.*

Support groups. Many times parents feel isolated and alone when they are having difficulties with their children or are facing problems in their personal lives. They may believe they are being bad parents. When coming together in support groups, the family members will find that others are dealing with similar issues and that they are not alone.

During the sessions, a facilitator helps the parents to support each other while they work to help themselves. Support groups can be organized around most any issue that is of concern to a group of parents. Some of the more common include single parenthood, living with middle-grade students, effects of divorce on children, grandparents raising grandchildren, drug and alcohol abuse, and dealing with unmotivated students.

Parent Abuse

A middle-school principal in San Jose, California, said one of the things she found that parents of young adolescents have had trouble dealing with is that their children often become physically or psychologically abusive to them. This remark seemed rather harsh, but it is probably true. As children reach this age, they are fighting for their independence and may push the parents away in the process.

I heard someone remark, when describing middle-school children, that they could understand why alligators eat their young. I'm certainly not suggesting anything that harsh, but middle-grade students are a different breed. However, organizing support groups for the parents can help them get through this difficult phase in their child's life.

Flexible locations. At times, the programs and activities should be offered in locations other than the school. Often the families' neighborhoods are located some distance from the school. Meetings, classes, workshops, and other events can be held at neighborhood churches, synagogues, community centers, hospitals, or businesses. Holding the sessions on the families' "home turf" is particularly important if the family members are not comfortable coming into the school.

The neighborhood locations will be less threatening and the parents will recognize that the school is reaching out to them. Once the parents are connected and feeling good about working with the faculty and staff, you can suggest that some of the meetings be held at the school.

Flexible meeting times. Be aware of the limitations placed on the families' time, (e.g., both parents are working, factory shifts, traffic, distances, etc.).

Schedule the workshops and classes at the most convenient times. Hold multiple sessions if one meeting time won't work for a lot of families.

Child care. Some families may not be able to attend because they lack child care. Recruit older students (especially those in child care-related classes), family members, and community volunteers to supervise the children. Child care is also a good opportunity for academic and social enrichment. Equip the area with educational toys, books, videos, and games. Schools can use some of their Title I funds to care for children during family/school meetings.

Transportation. Arrange transportation for families that have no means to get the sessions. Public transportation or school buses can be used to get the family to and from the meetings. Be cautious about using faculty or volunteers to transport parents because of liability considerations. Again, Title I funds can be used to transport parents to school if this is a barrier.

Language. If you anticipate that some of the parents do not speak English, present the sessions in their language or provide translators. This is very important with our diverse society. Schools can use Title I funds to provide translators.

Student invitations. Having the children write personal invitations asking the parents to attend classes, workshops, or support group sessions is often the little push that is needed. These invitations are likely to be art on the refrigerator door.

Parent recognition. Hopefully, the parents are attending because they are interested and feel their participation will help them and their children. Even so, people like to be recognized for their efforts. Little forms of recognition can sustain attendance and participation. There are many ways to recognize the parents' participation. For example:

- The names of family members attending classes and sessions are published in the school newsletter or read as part of the morning announcements.
- Group pictures are taken and submitted to the local newspaper for publication. Copies are also given to participants.
- Family members are given name tags at the opening meeting and are awarded a gold star for their tag when they attend subsequent sessions.
- Small, inexpensive door prizes are given at the end of the sessions. The schools may purchase the items, but often the prizes are donated by local business and agencies. Teachers and community members may be good sources. Most people have great prizes stored away in closets and drawers.
- Have an awards ceremony for the family members at the end of the year. Make sure that everyone gets an award of some kind.
- At the first session, conduct nonthreatening icebreaker activities designed to help people get acquainted.

Providing love, affection, and attention. When working with the family at school or in the home, encourage the parents to give each child abundant love, affection, and attention. Some of the outward demonstrations of love may change as the child grows older, but it is important to maintain a constant level of affection.

Even in situations where there is limited family time (e.g., a single parent, both parents working, many children in family, etc.), each child still needs some quality time with the parent. Help the families to plan their routines so each child gets the love, affection, and attention he or she needs.

Providing praise and approval. As with love, affection, and attention, it is crucial that each child is praised and shown approval. Even when the child's behavior does not live up to the family's expectations, the feedback needs to be given in a positive constructive manner.

Coach the parents how to avoid delivering their messages in a punitive or derogatory way. Making these adjustments in parent and child behavior often requires changes in the family culture. This is a developmental process and it takes time and effort.

Providing recognition and support. The children must get the message from the parent that education is important and that what they do in school is valued. To help with this process, coach the family members to:

- discuss with the children what they did each day in school and review papers, projects, and other materials that come home
- have a place in the home where the child's school work is displayed in a prominent place like on a bulletin board or on the refrigerator door
- share examples of the child's work, stories, poems, art work, and so forth, with relatives and friends; not only does this help the child, but grandparents, aunts, and uncles love to receive these "goodies" in the mail

ENHANCING THE PARENT PARTNER ROLES

Coaching the Nurturer Parent Partner Role

The goal of the Nurturer Parent Partner Role is to provide an appropriate environment where the child will flourish physically, psychologically, and emotionally. This role is concerned with the child's overall health, shelter, and safety, and encompasses the responsibility of maintaining positive learning conditions and environments at home. It is the most basic and fundamental Parent Partner Role.

When playing the Nurturer Role, it is expected fully involved parents will:

- offer love, praise, and encouragement
- support the child's education by providing an appropriate learning environment
- provide day-to-day necessities, school supplies and equipment, medical examinations, vaccinations, and so on
- regulate television use, schedule daily homework times, and establish family learning and living routines
- respond to the school's request for registration forms, schedules, report card signatures, permission slips, and other information
- monitor the child's in-school attendance and behavior and out-of-school activities
- enroll the child in enrichment programs such as dance, music and art lessons, after-school sports, and community recreational programs
- encourage the child to participate in religious services and youth groups

Nurturer Role Workshops and Class Topics

A variety of workshops and classes can be offered to enhance parents' Nurturer Role skills and knowledge. Such sessions focus on ways the family members can help themselves and the children while improving the living and learning conditions in the home. For example, a "How to Survive Mornings" workshop can provide the parents with strategies to prepare for the early morning rush.

The strategies includes things the family and child can do the night before to help the morning go smoother, such as choosing and laying out clothes, packing lunches, placing book bags by door, setting the table for breakfast, and so on. The following are other examples of workshops and classes to enhance the Nurturer Role. The examples are organized under "How To" or "Question and Answer" session categories.

"How To" Workshops and Classes

Many parents need to enhance their skills and knowledge in dealing with the crises and pressures of family life. The "How To" sessions offer strategies and information in this area. Some "how to" examples are:

- build relationships between siblings and other family members
- improve your child's feelings and attitudes toward school
- discipline your child

- find and get a job
- locate and work with support agencies in the community (e.g., department of social services)
- apply for unemployment benefits, food stamps, social security, job training, and so on
- locate and select a day care program
- get your electricity, gas, or telephone service restored
- make birthing arrangements
- sustain hope in the face of long-term adversity
- increase control over your life
- be a good role model
- overcome social isolation
- relax and reduce stress
- eat healthy and control your weight
- deal with grief and loss
- build self-esteem and social skills
- make funeral arrangements
- maintain your car
- fix simple things around your home

The Lady in the Red Shoes

At a parent education class on how to find and get employment, the group members were working on their interview skills. One of the parents arrived for the role-playing session wearing bright red high heel shoes and a miniskirt. The other parents shared with her that maybe she should dress a little more conservatively for a job interview, and definitely not wear red shoes. Everyone laughed, and she accepted the suggestion with good humor.

"Question and Answer" Meetings

Many parents have never had the opportunity to talk informally with professionals and government officials about health care, social services, rules and regulations, health and safety, and other issues. For example, a dentist or a social service agency representative is invited to meet with the families for a "question and answer" session. The parents ask questions and receive information about services, resources, and prevention programs. In some cases, the parents may not know what questions to ask, so the guest tells them about his or her specialty. Question and answer meetings can feature sessions with a:

- dentist
- pediatrician

- lawyer
- public health nurse
- poison control center representative
- nutritionist
- fireman
- police officer
- drug abuse counselor
- mayor

The Birthing Experience

Often, when working with the families you discover that parents are not prepared to deal with the most fundamental issues. One time when I was observing a parent education meeting at a family center in Nashville, an event occurred that illustrates this point.

My friend, Sujette Overstreet, whom I mentioned earlier, was talking with a woman at the parent club. The parent was very pregnant. It was the woman's first baby and they were discussing the upcoming birth. During the conversation, the young woman revealed that she had never been in a hospital before. She did not know what was going to happen and was scared and apprehensive.

Her remark was especially poignant because it contrasted so much with another discussion I had experienced earlier in the day. At another school, I had overheard a pregnant teacher telling a colleague that she and her husband were trying to decide which type of birthing room to use. She was expecting her third child and was discussing the pros and cons of each alternative. It struck me that the two women were preparing for a similar event, yet each had vastly different agendas.

I shared this with Sujette, and she arranged for the two pregnant women to get together and talk. The teacher shared with the young mother-to-be what to expect when she went into labor and gave birth. Sujette took the young woman to the hospital to visit the maternity ward. Because of these interventions, although still anxious, the new parent-to-be was much better prepared for the blessed event.

This scenario illustrates how families may need help in the most basic areas. Many parents do not have skills and knowledge, nor experiences that are typically taken for granted.

Nurturer Role Coaching Best Practices

Parents' and kids' sports night. Professional and college athletes are invited to come to talk with the parents and students about the importance of education. The evening can include videos of the athlete's highlights, prizes, and autographs. The kids and parents love to have their picture taken with the athletes.

Monitor television and computer games. There are numerous studies and articles that indicate that too much television is detrimental to the child's social and academic development. Studies also show that children who watch educational programs rather than general programs have higher reading scores.

Therefore, work with the parents to help them regulate how much time the children spend watching television and playing computer games, and what programs they watch. Regulating computer game and television content is important. Suggest which programs are available that are most helpful to the children. Include a list of programs in a newsletter or on a school website.

Contracts, covenants, and compacts. Written agreements between the families and the school can help build relationships to support education. The agreements are referred to as "contracts," "covenants," or "compacts." I believe the names are synonymous.

On the surface, having the families and the school sign a contract that pledges cooperation and outlines the responsibilities of each partner seems like a good plan. And it is, under the right conditions. However, you cannot legislate commitment any more than you can mandate involvement.

To get a family that is feeling disconnected with the school, to sign an agreement will be extremely difficult, if not impossible. Under those conditions, even if the family was to sign a contract, it would probably be meaningless. On the other hand, if the family is "connected" signing a covenant could be very useful. The contract has to be built on trust.

Below is an example of a family/school contract:

Parent/Family Member Agreement

(Any person who is interested in helping this student may sign in lieu of the parent.) I want my child to achieve. Therefore, I will encourage him/her by doing the following:

See that my child is punctual and attends school regularly.
Support the school in its efforts to maintain proper discipline.
Establish a time for homework and review it regularly.
Provide a quiet well-lighted place for study.
Encourage my child's efforts and be available for questions.
Be aware of what my child is learning.
Provide a library card for my child.
Read with my child and let my child see me read.

Respond to request for information from the school.
Initiate home-learning activities.
Continue to learn how to play my parenting role.

Signature_____

Student Agreement
It is important that I work to the best of my ability. Therefore, I shall strive to do the following:

Attend school regularly.
Come to school each day with pens, pencils, paper, and other necessary tools
    for learning.
Complete and return homework assignments.
Observe regular study hours.
Conform to rules of student conduct.
Be involved in home-learning activities

Signature_____

Teacher Agreement
It is important that students achieve. Therefore, I shall strive to do the following:

Provide regular homework assignments for students.
Provide necessary assistance to parents so that they can help with assign-
    ments and initiate home-learning activities.
Encourage students and parents by providing information about student
    progress.
Use special activities in the classroom to make learning enjoyable and
    meaningful.

Signature_____

Principal Agreement
I support this form of parent involvement. Therefore, I shall strive to do the following:

Work to establish positive two-way communication flows between the
    teacher, parent, and student.
Build collaborative relationships with the families.

Encourage teachers to regularly provide homework assignments and home-learning activities that will reinforce classroom instruction.

Implement strategies to help parents with their parenting skills and knowledge.

Signature_____

Coaching the Communicator Parent Partner Role

The goal of the Communicator Parent Partner Role is to communicate effectively with the child and the school. Usually, when the child is doing well at home and in school, there is a good communication flow between the family members and the child, and the parents and the school. On the other hand, when problems arise in the family or with the school, usually there is a breakdown in communications.

When playing the Communicator Role, it is expected that fully involved parents will:

- communicate with the child about successes in school and home, problems and concerns, and how they will support him or her in programs and activities
- communicate a strong sense of ethics and standards; high expectations; positive values; and character traits, such as respect, responsibility, hard work, and integrity
- know what is going on in the school life of the child
- maintain continuous communication with the school, especially about ways to support the child's learning
- monitor homework, projects, and other assignments
- dialogue with the school about the child's progress, strengths, and weaknesses
- participate in productive parent/teacher conferences
- respond promptly and effectively to letters and phone calls from school
- make timely and appropriate requests for information, assistance, and advice
- visit the school regularly and talk with teachers, counselors, and principals

Communicator Workshops and Class Topics

The workshops and classes are designed to enhance the family members' ability to communicate more effectively with their children and the school.

For example, the parents need to know how to obtain information from their child's teacher and other members of the school staff. They need to be able to find out how they can reinforce in the home what is happening in school, and what services, such as tutoring centers, homework hotlines, and community agencies, are available.

The following are other examples of workshops and classes to enhance the Communicator Role. The examples are organized under "How To" or "Question and Answer" session categories.

"How To" Workshops and Classes

Many parents need to enhance their communicating skills and knowledge. The "How To" sessions offer strategies and information in this area. Some "how to" examples are:

- find out what is going on in your child's school life
- help your child be successful in school
- prepare your child to take a test
- read report cards and student records
- monitor homework assignments
- give and receive constructive feedback
- understand the daily school schedule

"Question and Answer" Sessions

As with the Nurturer Role, many parents have never had the opportunity to talk informally with the principal, faculty, and other school officials about educational issues. Therefore, schedule meetings with the school's leadership team, faculty, and staff so family members can ask questions and become familiar with programs and services. The sessions can be held at school or in the neighborhoods depending upon the situation. Question and answer meetings can feature sessions with the:

- principal
- guidance counselor
- faculty members
- school nurse
- speech therapist
- Communities-in-Schools representative
- reading recovery teacher
- special education teacher or coordinator

Other Communicator Role Workshops and Class Topics

Workshops and classes that can be used to enhance the Communicator Role are:

- communicating with your child
- interpersonal facilitation skills
- parent-student-teacher conferences skills
- homework and homework skills
- standardized testing and other benchmark programs
- extracurricular activities and policies
- grading policies
- discipline policies
- availability of school support services
- prekindergarten and kindergarten parent orientation
- transitioning from elementary to middle school
- transitioning from middle to high school

Communicator Role Coaching Best Practices

The Communicating Strategy chapter (chapter 7) presents best practices the school can use to establish two-way communication flows with the families. Since the process is reciprocal, some of the program and activities included in chapter 8 can also help to enhance the parents' communication skills and knowledge.

Family discussions (dinner table talk). Many children, especially middle- and high-school students, report that they do not feel they communicate often enough with their parents. Encourage and help the families to schedule a time each day to discuss the happenings of the day with the children (e.g., what occurred in school, activities after school, etc.). Find a time when the whole family is together, like at the dinner table or other meal times. Family discussion times are great opportunities to tell stories, recount experiences, and share problem-solving strategies.

Parents may need help in conducting discussions with the children. For example, being a good listener is very important. Family members can be shown how to listen to their child's opinions as well giving their own.

Parent handbooks. Provide families with a handbook that includes information on topics that they need to know such as:

- school board policies
- school's mission and goals
- school regulations
- curriculum

- grade-level learning goals and objectives
- procedures for monitoring student progress
- grading and exam policy
- homework policy
- discipline policy
- attendance and tardy policy
- standardized testing program
- student and parent rights
- schedule for school events and programs
- visiting and volunteer opportunities

Include a directory and organizational plan that designates the persons responsible for the day-to-day operations of the school and school district. List the names of the faculty and staff and telephone numbers where they can be contacted at school.

Since the Communicator Role is a lower-order role, these best practices can be used to form a foundation for the higher-order roles. For example, the parents will need to know and understand the information in the parent handbook in order to mediate and negotiate for the child (Advocator Role).

Coaching the Teacher Parent Partner Role

The goal of the Teacher Partner Role is to assist with the child's moral, intellectual, emotional, and social development. The parent, or surrogate, is the child's first teacher and possibly the child's most important teacher. The effect the family has on the child, especially in the early years, is significant and dramatic.

The Nurturer and Communicator Parent Partner Roles provide the foundation for the teaching function. The Teacher Parent Partner Role builds on this foundation by working with the child to provide him or her with the basic skills and knowledge. When the missing families are not involved in the education of the children, it is the parents' inability to play the Teacher Partner Role that has the most negative impact on the children's development. By enhancing the parents' capacities to assume the Teacher Partner Role, more children will be better prepared for the schooling experience.

When playing the Teacher Role, it is expected that fully involved parents will do the following:

- Initiate learning activities or respond to the child's requests for help.
- Work with the teachers to coordinate the child's classroom work with home-based learning activities.
- Meet with teachers to make home-learning materials and learn how to teach particular skills and knowledge (e.g., reading, writing, math).

- Engage the children in family games that relate to school work and home learning.
- Utilize instructional techniques designed to help children with homework and other projects and activities.
- Expose the child to various cultural, career, scientific, and historic sites, events, and programs.
- Select creative and educational television programs that the families watch together, and discuss.
- Depending on the age of the child, read to the child, have the child read to you, read together; and ensure that the child reads alone.
- Praise the child's work.
- Take the child to the library to select books, videos, and CDs.
- Use "make-and-take" educational aides and materials made at family/school sessions.

Teacher Workshop and Class Topics

Schedule workshops and classes to help family members learn how to teach and work with their children at home. Faculty, curriculum coordinators, and other resource personnel can be enlisted to conduct the sessions. Organize the workshops and classes so that different teaching strategies are demonstrated and modeled. When appropriate, ask the families to bring the children to the sessions so they can practice with their own children.

"How To" Workshops and Classes

The "How To" sessions offer strategies and information in this area. Some "how to" examples are:

- motivate your child
- help children learn
- build self-esteem in your child
- read a book to a child
- have a child read to you
- use home-learning activities
- improve your child's skills in reading, math, writing, and other subjects
- develop a home reading program

Other Teacher Role Workshop and Class Topics

Workshops and classes that can be used to enhance the Teacher Role are:

- study skills
- math and literacy skills by grade levels

- creating summer learning opportunities
- songs and finger plays
- teaching math, reading, writing, science, social studies, and so on
- computer skills

Coaching the Use of Home-Learning Activities

Helping the parents with the use of home-learning activities is probably the most important best practice to enhance the Teacher Roles. Many of the workshops and class topics listed above relate to home-learning activities. However, because this area is so important, this section presents an array of suggestions for enhancing the parents' abilities to work with their children on home-learning activities.

Opportunities for home learning can occur anywhere and at any time. Learning can happen when you are doing the dishes, driving the car, shopping, putting the children to bed, or sitting watching television. The interactions the parents have with their children, especially during the younger years, play a major role in literacy and math basic skill development. Urge the families to make the most of the time they have with their children by looking for teachable moments and conducting home-learning activities.

Coach parents to:

- make reading a part of the daily family routine by reading to young children at least twenty minutes a day.
- have older children read to you each day.
- make it a practice to have the child read or read to them before going to bed. On weekends, as a special treat, let the child stay up a little later and read in bed.
- discuss with the child the books read to them or that the child has read.
- when reading a poem, ask the child to guess what the next rhyming word may be.
- ask the child to think if the content of the book relates to him or experiences he has had.
- ask the child how he or she might have changed the story, or before finishing a story, ask the child how he or she thinks it will end.
- tell stories about your childhood, family life, vocations, hobbies, and dreams.
- keep good books, magazines, and newspapers in the house.
- serve as a role model by reading at least 30 minutes yourself. It might be difficult to fit this into busy schedules, but effort can pay off for you and the child.

- always have books available in the car for long road trips and traffic delays and to read in restaurants when waiting to be served.
- have the child read the map when traveling.
- vary the daily reading settings (e.g., read under a tree in the yard or at a nearby park).
- have reciprocal spelling bees where the child gives you a word and the child checks, then you give the child a word, and you check it together.
- teach the older child how to use and read the newspaper. Show them the different sections and where to find such things as a summary of the headlines, sports scores, the weather report, entertainment schedules, and horoscopes. Give the child a list of local and national headlines and have them locate where the headlines are printed.
- look through a catalog and newspaper ads, especially the Sunday inserts, and identify common household items (e.g., sports equipment, clothing, etc.). Have the child practice reading and saying the names of the items. Also, cut the names of items out of the catalog or newspaper and tape them on the real items around the house. Again, have the child read the names and identify the objects.
- use a newspaper or magazine to work with the child and find all the "A's," "B's," and so on, or certain words like, "that," "which," "when," "many." Ask older children to find nouns, adverbs, adjectives, and so forth.
- give the child a ruler, yardstick, and measuring tape and ask him or her to measure things around the house, the size of rooms, chairs, television sets, kitchen table, and so on. Have the child measure the heights of her brothers and sisters, and her height.
- talk with the child about time (e.g., A.M. and P.M., positions on a clock face, hours in a day, etc.). Have him practice telling time and adding and subtracting times of day.
- have the child read the recipe or the directions on the package when you are cooking and have the child measure out the ingredients. Discuss how the different amounts relate to each other. Talk about how you would double or triple a recipe. Have the child see how many cups of water fit into a quart jar, how many teaspoons of sugar in one tablespoon, and so forth.
- have the child read the labels and determine the weight and size when putting groceries and other supplies away.
- talk about the groceries and supplies that you buy at the store. Discuss where certain foods are grown (e.g., bananas, grapes, apples); what some products are made of and why they work the way they do (e.g., detergents, glass cleaners, etc.).

- help the child to notice things when walking or driving in the neighbor-hood, at a park, in the city, out in the country, or other places. Discuss where they are, what they are seeing and hearing, and what is happening.
- show the child what you are buying in the grocery markets and other stores and how to compare prices of similar items. Show the child the price-by-unit labels on the shelves beneath the products, and ask the child to name the items.
- ask the child to read the signs and posters displayed in stores.
- limit television viewing to no more than two hours a day. This should apply to everyone. Parents should set an example.
- find a television program that everyone enjoys and watch it together. Discuss what happened; the meaning of the program; what was funny, sad, boring, unrealistic, and so forth.
- have the child write as much as possible. This can include such things as telephone messages, letters, diaries, and grocery lists.
- discuss with the child the nature of tides and tide tables when you are near the ocean. Have the child keep track of the changes in tides during a week.

Family Math

The Lawrence Hall of Science at the University of California, Berkeley, has developed a program that brings parents and children together to learn about mathematics. The program, originally funded from a grant by the U.S. Department of Education, gives parents and children (kindergarten through grade 8) opportunities to develop problem-solving skills and to build an understanding of mathematics using hands-on materials. Manipulatives like blocks, beans, pennies, and toothpicks are used to help children to understand mathematical concepts such as numbers and space. Family Math topics include arithmetic, geometry, probability and statistics, computers, and logic. It is not a remedial program. The emphasis is on the families having fun as they learn together and parents get involved in their children's math education.

A typical Family Math course includes six or eight sessions of an hour or two. The classes are usually scheduled in the evening (6:30 P.M–8:30 P.M.) or on weekends. The families are given overviews of the mathematics topics at their children's grade levels and explanations of how these topics relate to each other. To ensure that the reason for studying mathematics is clear, men and women working in math-based occupations come to some of the sessions and talk about how they use math in their jobs. Usually, light refreshments are served, and sometimes schools have door prizes and surprise awards. Families are recognized in some way for their involvement (e.g., certificates, T-shirts, badges, bumper stickers, etc.). For more information contact: Lawrence Hall of Science, University of California at Berkley, CA 94702, (510) 642-5132, or ihsweb@berkley.edu.

MegaSkills

My dear friend, Dr. Dorothy Rich, who passed away in 2009, was the director and founder of the Home and School Institute, a long-time proponent of family and school partnerships, and her publications on home-learning activities are internationally known. Her program called "MegaSkills" (1988a) is about academic and social development. Dorothy was always on the cutting edge, and the MegaSkills program combines her home recipe approach with what is now being called "character education." The "MegaSkills" are what she called, "inner-engines of learning." (They are confidence, motivation, effort, responsibility, initiative, perseverance, caring, teamwork, common sense, and problem-solving.)

The MegaSkills program is designed to help both students and parents. Rich reported that after participating in the program, children and adults are more proactive and "feel more in charge of their lives, more resilient in the force of adversity, and better able to take advantage of opportunities." The program is an excellent Coaching Strategy best practice. For more information, contact Dorothy Rich Associates, Inc. 1500 Massachusetts Ave., NW Washington, DC 20005; (202) 362-7889 or megaskills.org.

Teacher Role Coaching Best Practices

Field Trips. Many parents have never visited the places where their children typically go on class field trips such as the library, fire stations, museum, zoo, hospital, and so forth. Encourage the teachers to invite the family members to join their children on these field trips.

The school can also organize and conduct trips just for the families. By experiencing the different sites, the parents are better able to help their children use the field trips as learning experiences.

A Scavenger Hunt

A family/school coordinator in a rural community near Chattanooga, Tennessee, made a field trip a family learning experience by adding a scavenger hunt to the event. A trip to downtown Chattanooga was planned for the parents and children. Most of the family members had never visited any of the sites and many had not been downtown.

Prior to the trip, the coordinator took photographs of some of things the families and children would be expected to see on the trip. She took pictures of buildings that were the focus of the trip: the museum, library, and aquarium. She also photographed more common objects such as pieces of outdoor sculpture, clocks, unusual signs, a bus stop shelter, and a manhole cover. The coordinator made enough copies of the pictures so that each family would have a set. Before leaving on the trip, she gave the parents and children the pictures along with a check list. They were instructed to check off an item when they found the subject shown in a photograph. During the field trip, the families enjoyed the scavenger hunt and learned a lot in the process.

Libraries. Encourage parents to take the children to the library on a regular basis to check out books, videos, and educational software. Make sure the family members have library cards and know how to check out items. If some families are not familiar with the location and use of the library, conduct a tour after school or on a weekend. As noted earlier, if a visit to the library is a classroom field trip, invite the family members to go along.

Suggest that on the occasions when their child asks them a question they cannot answer, take him or her to the library to find the answer. It will be an opportunity to find the answer to the question and at the same time learn a lesson in the use and value of the library.

Family toy and game libraries. Establish programs for lending educational and creative toys, computer software, puzzles, books, video and audio tapes, and games to the families for home-learning activities. Locate the toy and game libraries in the school or community. The programs are often supervised by parents and community volunteers.

Computer loan programs. Establish a computer and software loan program to help families with home-learning activities. Training is provided by school staff and volunteers. Programs like this can help reduce the gap between the computer literate "haves" and "have nots." Money to buy equipment and software and run the programs often come from grants, private donations, and Title 1 funds.

Computers in the Home

The Buddy System Project in Indiana began in 1988 with the purpose to place a computer in the home of every 4–12 grade student. The intent was to extend learning beyond the classroom and to ensure equal access for all children in Indiana to the many resources and advantages afforded in the information age. Now called Buddy2, it still maintains its original core values, but has responded to the rapid changes in educational technology.

The program serves the Indiana schools, teachers, students, and their families with quality materials, training, and support in integrating technology in education. For more information contact: the Buddy Project, 6920 Gatwick Drive, Suite 130, Indianapolis, IN 46241, (317) 856) 22223 or BuddyProject.org.

A Literacy Night with Dr. Seuss. In March, the Hill Field Elementary School in Utah held an evening event called, "A Literacy Night with Dr. Seuss." The students and parents were invited to arrive in pajamas for Dr. Seuss' "birth-day party." The principal dressed up as the notable character, and the faculty and staff appeared as the Cat in the Hat, the Grinch, the Thing One and Thing Two, and other Dr. Seuss characters. The characters greeted and met with the families and played games.

The evening included read-out-loud stories, reading with families, and storytelling. Cake and punch were served and the evening concluded with the singing of "Happy Birthday" to Dr. Seuss. All students received a packet with a free book and other literacy materials such as bookmarks and information about the public library.

"Make-And-Take" parties. Hold sessions where parents come to the school to make or produce home-learning materials. The teachers show the family members how to make the activity, and how to use it with their children. The learning activities usually relate to the children's school work. The school supplies the paper, crayons, glue, glitter, feathers, and other materials. Sometimes the children join the family members at the workshop.

An example is a "Make-a-Book Workshop." The parents work together to create a book for each child in the family. The family members make up stories, write them down, make illustrations, and put the pages together in a book. When finished, the books are taken home and read to the children.

Another example is a "Tote Bag" party. The parents make tote bags for a reading project. The school or PTA buys books for the children to check out and they carry the books back and forth in the tote bags.

The "Make-and-Take" parties can be scheduled around holidays such as Halloween, Thanksgiving, or Mother's Day. The families make things that can be used to celebrate and learn about the holiday. Some schools have found funds to pay teachers to conduct "Make-and-Take" parties during the summer as part of their summer "shady tree" enrichment programs.

A nice touch is to take pictures of the families with their creations. One copy of the photograph can be given to the family and another can be displayed in the child's classroom.

Have toys, will travel. Establish programs that take the educational materials to the homes. Paid or nonpaid volunteers bring a toy or games for the week, month, etc. Parents are shown how to use the toy or game and are instructed on how it relates to the child's academic or social development. Each time a home visit is made, a new toy or game is exchanged for the previous one.

Community arts fair. Community artists can be invited to come to school, probably on a Saturday, to demonstrate music, dance, painting, pottery, and other crafts. Musicians from the community can perform. Students can perform and display their art as well. This is a great way to support the arts.

Family educational plans. Help the families to develop collaborative educational plans for working with the children at home. Goals and objectives can be established and strategies can be outlined. Teachers can send weekly activities to help coordinate the home learning with the child's schoolwork.

Television contracts. All members of a family sign a contract stating that the television will be unplugged or turned off for a period of time (i.e., a week, month, etc.). The families are given communication strategies and home-learning activities, in reading, writing, math, and other subjects. Books and educational toys are made available for the families to check out. With the popularity of computer games, the families agree to use the computer only for educational purposes during the period of time.

Family study nights. Schedule family study nights two evenings per week at schools, churches, synagogues, and community centers. These two- or three-hour sessions provide a quiet place for students and family members to work together on school work or enrichment tasks.

The study nights are a structured way to get away from the television, computer games, and other distractions. Usually teachers, parents, or community volunteers are available to act as resources. Snacks and refreshments are provided to help make the sessions more relaxed and enjoyable.

Saturday enrichment day. This activity is a variation of the family study night. Parents and children meet on a Saturday morning to work together on a high-interest learning activity. The sessions should be fun and fast moving to ensure that the families attend.

Saturday school. Four-year-olds receive home visits and attend a 3-hour session in school on Saturdays. Parents assist the teachers during the sessions. All parents receive a weekly guide to home-based learning activities and other ideas for things the families can do together during the week.

Family teaching resource directory. A directory is compiled that describes school and community teaching resources available to families. The directory lists such things as family reading and language centers, museums, nature centers, and libraries. Copies of the directory are distributed to the families and school personnel. The directory can also be placed on the school's website. Again, be sensitive to the reality that not all parents are computer savvy.

School bus classrooms and parenting centers. The first time I ran across a program that used converted school buses to reach out to children and parents was in Murfreesboro, Tennessee. The program placed the mobile learning centers in low-income neighborhoods to increase the language and concept development of at-risk three- and four-year-old children and to enhance the parents' commitment to help with their children's education.

The "learning centers" were two school buses that were no longer being used to transport children because of a state total mileage law. Although they could not be used for their original purpose of moving children, the buses could be driven from place to place by adults. The buses were in reasonably good condition and were remodeled for the project—the bench seats were removed, and lights, air conditioning, heating, tables, shelves, chairs, and so forth were added.

Each bus was supplied with preschool equipment and materials. A teacher and an aide were assigned to each mobile classroom and drove the buses around the city to certain sites to offer the program. After plugging into an electrical and water supply, the classrooms were ready for business.

Groups of neighborhood children would come to the buses for instruction. An individual child visited the bus twice a week for about two hours. The sessions included group learning activities, free time to play with educational toys, and other learning activities. Materials were also sent home each week for the child and parent to work on together. Local radio stations, newspapers, and personal contracts were used to make the public aware of the program. Funding sources for the program came from the local school board, civic organizations, church groups, and individual contributions.

This program was an excellent way to use old equipment in a most productive way. It provided a way to establish an instructional and parenting center in the several neighborhoods at the same time. I have found a variety of programs that use mobile units to reach families. Besides being used as classrooms, mobile units also house family resource centers, health clinics, and social service centers.

Pump Bus

In Syracuse, NY, there is a PUMP (Power Unit for Motivating Parents) bus that reaches out to parents in the evenings and weekends during nonwinter months (yes, it does snow in Syracuse). The bus is staffed by the school district's parent advocate and three parent liaisons. The PUMP bus seeks out the parents where it can find them (e.g. community shopping centers, cultural festivals, outside city hall). The focus of the program is to support at-home learning and assist parents to help their children to meet the state's learning standards in literacy and math.

Preschool screening programs. The school and social agencies collaborate to screen young children before they enter prekindergarten or kindergarten programs. The purposes of the screening programs are twofold: (1) to identify potential problem areas and (2) to train parents to work with the children to remediate the identified problem areas. The goal is for the children to arrive at school in the fall ready for their classes.

The school district in Athens, Tennessee, offers a program where the physical screenings are conducted by the county health department. The physical screening includes physical examination, immunization, blood work, urinalysis, weight and height, and vision and hearing tests. The children are also screened in the educational and developmental areas to determine strengths and weaknesses.

The screening informs the teachers about deficiencies and problem areas. The children are administered the LAP-D, DIAL-R, *Gessell School Readiness Test, Battelle Developmental Inventory,* or other similar instruments. A profile is developed and the results are used by the kindergarten, or preschool, teachers and parents to plan an educational program to remedy problem areas. The screenings occur in June, with a make-up screening day scheduled in September.

A "Parent Day" is held in the early summer where the parents come to school to learn what they can do to help prepare the children for school through at-home learning activities. When needed, provisions are also made for parents and families to counsel with school and agency personnel, such as the school psychologist and speech therapists.

The media is used to disseminate information about the screening activities and training. After school starts, teachers use newsletters, notes, telephone calls, and letters to continue the intervention.

This program involves the families and builds partnerships before the children enter school. The parents and teachers work together from the beginning to help ensure that the children will have a successful school experience. Other best practices for coordinating services and resources, such as school-based family resource and service centers, are presented in the Coordinating Strategy chapter (chapter 8).

Coaching the Supporter Parent Partner Role

The goal of the Supporter Parent Partner Role is to be actively supportive of the child's and the school's activities and programs. While the role is both school- and child-directed, it is played in the school environment. Providing support to the child in the home is one of the functions the Nurturer Parent Partner Role.

This role is a middle-level role, and it is assumed that the family members are already playing their lower-level roles. I want to emphasize again that the term "lower order" does not apply to the importance of the role, but rather to the need to be able to master them before the upper-level roles can be assumed. In fact, the Nurturer, Communicator, and Teacher roles are probably the most crucial of all the roles.

The programs and activities that are implemented to enhance the Supporter Role are designed to strengthen the "families supporting the school" aspect of the partnership. However, it is expected that the parents are involved with the child's education at home (Nurturer and Teacher Roles) and that they know and understand what is going on in school (Communicator Role).

When playing the Supporter Role, it is expected that fully involved parents will:

- participate in classroom events, open houses, and PTA/PTO programs
- attend school concerts, plays, award assemblies, sport events, and other productions
- assist teachers, administrators, and children in the classrooms and in other areas of the school
- participate in booster clubs and other fund-raising activities
- chaperone field trips and dances
- organize and conduct campus cleanups and beautification projects

Supporter Workshops and Class Topics

Since the family members should already know about the school's curriculum, programs and activities at this stage, the workshops and classes concentrate on such activities as volunteering, tutoring, mentoring, and so forth.

"How To" Workshops and Classes

The "How To" sessions offer strategies and information in this area. Some "how to" examples are:

- be a classroom volunteer
- tutor in science and math
- be a mentor
- work with special-needs children
- organize fund-raising projects
- supervise students at social events and on field trips

Other Supporter Role Coaching Best Practices

Daughter and dad dance. A best practice to help build support for the child and the school is a daughter and dad dance. The school holds a dance in the evening and invites the dads to bring their daughters to the event. There is DJ and refreshments are served. This is a way to get the dads involved with the school and it is a special event for all involved, especially the daughters. This is most appropriate for the upper grades in an elementary school. Daughters in middle and high school would probably not see going to a dance with their dads as "cool."

Men make a difference day. "Men Make a Difference Day" is an event where male role models (fathers, grandfathers, uncles, and other male figures) are invited to school. During the day, the men are briefed on school programs, tour the school, and participate in study groups to discuss what they as male role models can do to affect the lives of children. The goal is to increase the number of fathers and other male figures involved with the school.

There is a celebration at the end to recognize the participants. The day should be a fun learning event. In some cases, an abbreviated program can be held in the evening if the men are not available during the day.

Coaching the Learner Parent Partner Role

The goal of the Learner Parent Partner Role is to obtain new skills and knowledge that will help directly and indirectly with the child's educational and social development. While ultimately the family members' learning is directed at the child, the obtainment of new skills and knowledge will also help the parents with their own educational and social development.

The assumption is that by enhancement of the parents' general skills and knowledge, they will be better able to support their children and be involved in their education. The federal Even Start program is based on this notion. The program requires that the parents be enrolled in classes such as GED preparation, literacy, English as a second language, parenting, and so forth, when their children are in school or in the program's daycare center. The parents generally eat breakfast and lunch with their children and sometime during the day they work with the children on learning activities.

While the Learner Role encompasses all of the program and activities that are implemented to enhance the Parent Partner Roles, the best practices included in this section focus primarily on the parents' growth, which in turn, will help the child.

When playing the Learner Role, it is expected that fully involved parents will:

- participate in parent education programs that focus on such things as child development, parenting skills, alcohol and drug abuse, and teenage pregnancy
- obtain and read materials on such topics as school curriculum and activities, school board policies, school rules and regulations, basic skill development, parent and student rights, college preparation, and drop-out prevention
- enroll in adult education classes to improve general knowledge and skills in such areas as math, language, geography, education issues, reading, and literature

Learner Workshops and Class Topics

There is a vast array of workshops and classes that can be offered to enhance the family members' skills and knowledge. Some examples of parent education topics are:

- computer and Internet skills
- GED preparation program
- reading and basic literacy
- math
- English as a second language (ESL)
- foreign language
- human development
- adolescent behavior
- ages and stages in child development
- special health needs of children
- drug and alcohol awareness
- gang influence
- AIDS awareness and prevention
- sex education
- teenage pregnancy

Other Learner Role Coaching Best Practices

This section presents some examples of unusual programs and activities that can be used to enhance the parents' skills and knowledge. The best practices reflect a high expectation that the family members will respond positively to learning opportunities.

Snow White, a Parent Play

My wife, Jan, who was teaching at an inner-city school in Nashville read in the newspaper that a consultant had been hired by the district to work on a special project with gifted and talented students. The plan was for the consultant to spend a week with the students and have them learn a play. At the end of the week, the class would present the play to the whole school.

After reading the article, my wife had an idea and went to her principal and family/school coordinator. She said to the principal and coordinator, "Let's see if the consultant would come to our school and work with our families."

"Most of our family members have not completed high school and I'm sure they have never been in a play, but I think it is a great idea. Let's give it a try," the coordinator replied.

The principal agreed, and went to the district office to see if the consultant could come to the school to help the families put on a play for the children. Permission was granted, and arrangements were made.

The parents and faculty worked feverishly with the consultant for a week and on Friday presented "Snow White and the Seven Dwarfs." The play was presented as a satire. The family members made the scenery and props, including a giant candy kiss made out of aluminum wrap. The play was wonderful and the children loved it. After the performance, the school held a celebration for the families. Refreshments were served, and each family member received a rose and a certificate.

It was a new experience for the families who were very excited and proud. The family members experienced success because the coordinator and teachers had high expectations for them. They thought the family members could do it, and they did. Performing in the play was a life-changing experience for at least one parent. The woman who played Snow White assumed the name "Snow" after the play. Soon after the performance, she enrolled in classes at the community college to finish her hospital aide's training. She said that being in the play inspired her to return to school. After completing the hospital aide program, she got a job and moved out of the housing projects.

The following year, without the aid of the consultant, the parents and the faculty presented "Peter Rabbit." At the celebration party following the successful presentation, the family members gathered around the television to watch a video of their performance. They squealed in delight when they saw themselves on the screen. "What are we going to do next year?" they asked.

Parent Academy

Recently, I was working with a low-performing inner-city elementary school in Charlotte, North Carolina, to help them build a family/school partnership program. There had been virtually no parent involvement when I started. After implementing various connecting and communication strategies, collaborative relationships between the school and the parents were being established. We began having family night meals followed with high-interest events (e.g. student performances, music groups, professional athlete appearances, and such).

Then, building on these beginning events, family night meals were followed by interesting meetings on such topics as "ways to help their children with schoolwork." These meetings evolved into what we called the Parent Academy. Parent Academy meetings were scheduled at least once a month. The parents were surveyed to determine what topics were of interest. The parents expressed an interest in topics such as helping their children to read, the end-of-year testing, and disciple skills.

These meetings were popular, and eventually, sub-groups were established where family members attended classes in computer training, job interview skills, and GED preparation. Study groups were established to discuss such topics as diversity, discipline, and such. Since we were starting from scratch, it took about a year and a half to get to the "attending class" stage.

Parent university. The Charlotte-Mecklenburg Schools has partnered with community agencies and organizations to offer free courses, family events, and activities that will equip parents with "new or additional skills, knowledge, resources, and confidence." These events are help in schools, public libraries, YMCAs, houses of worship, businesses, and other community locations.

The goal is to help parents become full partners in their children's education. I think this best practice has the potential of being a successful program. However, in order to involve the hard-to-reach families, there has to be an effort to build relationships with the parents using connecting and communicating best practices. Without reaching out to these families, it is unlikely that they will attend.

Annual Family Affair

An elementary school in Charlotte, North Carolina, organized and hosted an event each October called the Annual Family Affair. It was an evening of family workshops combined with food, fun, and fellowship.

The Family Affair begins with a free supper (hot dogs, coleslaw, baked beans, dessert, and drinks) prepared by the cafeteria staff for the whole family. Over the years, organizations such as at&t, Belk Department Stores, and others have covered the cost of the meal and some of their employees have helped with the serving. Free transportation is provided if needed. Bus transportation and meal reservation forms are sent home with the children.

During supper, there is usually an inexpensive raffle ($1 per ticket) to raise money to support programs for the children and the families. The prizes included such items as two tickets to a professional basketball or football game, entertainment coupon book, sports jackets, and money. In addition to the raffle, door prizes are given out.

After dinner, the family members selected a workshop to attend and the children went to the multipurpose room and other classrooms, by age groups, for games and activities such as bean toss, cakewalk, basketball shoot, and go fish. The teachers and assistants organized and conducted the games and activities. The children received small inexpensive prizes. Babies and younger children were cared for by teachers and volunteers in a separate room.

To bridge the time between supper and the start of the workshops, the school arranged activities such as a police officer showing off his or her "drug-sniffing" dog and a clown making balloon animals for the children.

The PTA had a membership and a sale table where parents could join the organization and purchase school T-shirts and sweatshirts. The workshops were fast-moving and lasted no more than one hour. PTA members and families were asked what sort of session would be helpful and interesting.

A committee comprising the counselor, Communities-in-School representative, principal, assistant principal, PTA president, and teachers decided on the topics and identified individuals to lead the workshops. The following are some examples of workshops that were offered:

- Coping with homelessness—Homelessness is affecting more and more people each year. This workshop discusses services available to assist families overcoming homelessness and explore community resources.
- Positive discipline—The workshop coaches parents on how to discipline without using corporal punishment and how to teach children responsibility, cooperation, and problem-solving skills.
- Health education curriculum—This session is designed primarily for parents of 5th- and 6th-grade students. The program's parent handbook is used to guide the participants through a discussion of the components of the comprehensive Health Education instructional program (e.g., Family Living, Ethical Behavior, and Human Sexuality).
- Our reading program—The SRA Direct Instruction reading program is discussed. The parents are shown ways they can help their child be a better reader.
- PETALS (Parents Exploring Teaching and Learning Styles)—PETALS is a system of evaluations and activities that connects the parents with the child's learning processes. The workshop presented information on how children learn and shows the parents how to be a positive influence in their child's life.

The Annual Family Affair was a comprehensive family/school partnership strategy. The event employed Connecting best practices to reach out to the families, Communicating best practices to communicate effectively, Coordinating best practices to combine resources, and Coaching best practices to enhance the parents' skills and knowledge. The Annual Family Affair is a good example of an activity that demonstrates the commitment the faculty and staff have made to establishing and maintaining partnerships between the families and school.

Each year, the parents looked forward to the event and a high percentage of the total family population participated. The Family Affair did not just happen. It took a lot of work and the event grew and matured over the many years. Unfortunately, it is no longer held at the school.

With the changing of the principal, the event was discontinued. The demise of this successful event illustrates the need for the family/school partnership program to be part of the school's mission. With a strong mission statement, a new principal should be able to examine existing strategies that adhere to what the school is suppose to be about, rather than to start from scratch.

Survival Skills Program

One day, when I arrived at an inner-city elementary school, the family/ school coordinator and a group of parents were practicing for a graduation ceremony. The parents were "graduating" from a program called, "Survival Skills for Women." The 10 women had been attending this self-help training program developed by Dr. Linda P. Thurston of Survival Skills Education and Development (SSED). (There is a similar program for men.)

The program was designed to be presented as a series of 10 three-hour workshops. The topics of the workshops were: assertiveness, personal health, nutrition, money management, child management, self-advocacy, legal rights, coping with crisis, community resources, and re-entry/employment. The goal of the program was to empower the participants with the confidence and competence to have positive attitudes and beliefs in self, and to take charge of their external world.

The women were all single mothers on welfare who were living in the public housing complex that surrounded the school. The parents were reading at a third-grade level or below. After completing the survival program, they were encouraged to take basic literacy classes and enroll in a GED preparation program.

The graduation ceremony was an important conclusion to the training. The coordinator used the activity to recognize the women's accomplishments and to provide them with the opportunity to affirm their sense of empowerment.

The rehearsal was being held in the school's gym/auditorium. I was the only adult observer (three children rode tricycles across the old, but shiny hardwood floor). The coordinator coached the women on their speeches. One by one, they approached the lectern and read their statements. The women said such things as:

- *"Once I was passive, now I am assertive."*
- *"I learned how to stand up for my rights."*
- *"I did not expect to learn so much, so fast."*
- *"I learned to be more assertive, rather than aggressive."*

The next day the women, wearing caps and gowns, graduated before the entire student body. Each parent received a rose along with her diploma. The graduation speaker congratulated them on their accomplishments and

encouraged them to continue with their education. A reception with refresh-
ments followed the ceremony and the women continued to beam and smile as
they had throughout the day. This was a big event in their lives.

The impact of self-help workshops can be dramatic. Whether you purchase
a program or design your own, rituals and ceremonies are an important
aspect of the training. The recognition and praise will help to reinforce the
concepts presented in the program. For more information contact: SSED,
2007 Yanceyville Street, Box 46, Greensboro, NC 27406. (336) 272-4027 or
www.SSED.org.

Coaching the Advisor Parent Partner Role

The goal of the Advisor Parent Partner Role is to wisely counsel and advise
the child about personal and educational issues. Playing this role, the parent advises the child, rather than tells the child what to do. Since this is a
higher-order role, to be effective the family member and child need to be
able to communicate (Communicator Role) and to have a trusting relationship
(Nurturing Role).

Because the Advisor Role builds on the other Parent Partner Roles, the best
practices to enhance this role are focused and specific. It is assumed that, if
needed, the parents have been coached to play the lower-order roles.

When playing the Advisor Role, it is expected that fully involved parents
will:

- help with personal concerns and problems
- assist with curriculum and program issues
- advise about potential career paths and opportunities
- be familiar with contents of the student's records
- know and understand school procedures such as the standardized testing
  process, school-to-work homework activities, and so forth

Advisor Workshops and Class Topics

Some examples of workshop and class topics to enhance the Advisor Role
are:

- advising skills
- the helping relationship and counseling
- school-to-work programs
- applying to college
- financial aid and career planning

Other Advisor Role Coaching Best Practices

Since this is a higher-order role, it is important to assess the families and determine if they have skills and knowledge of such areas as:

- school board policies
- the school's mission and goals
- school regulations
- the school's curriculum
- grade-level learning goals and objectives
- procedures for monitoring student progress
- grading and exam policy
- homework policy
- discipline policy
- attendance and tardy policy
- standardized testing program
- student and parent rights
- college application procedures

Best practices found in the Communicator Parent Role section in this chapter and in the Communicating Strategy chapter (chapter 7) are implemented if it is determined that some areas need to be enhanced.

Career and college night. Schedule and host a Career and College Night at the school. Invite representatives from local colleges and universities, businesses and industries, government and social agencies and professions to talk with the families and students. Have guidance counselors available to answer questions.

Field trips to local colleges and corporations. Organize field trips for the parents and students to visit the local colleges and corporations. The families tour the facilities and learn about programs, products, and opportunities. Representatives from the different organizations are available to answer questions.

College student/family night. When local college students are home on vacation, invite them to the school for a meeting with interested students and parents. The college students answer questions and talk to the families about what they need to do to prepare for college.

Coaching the Advocator Parent Partner Role

The goal of the Advocator Role is to effectively and actively advocate, mediate, and negotiate for the child. Like the Supporter Role, this is generally played in the school setting. Specific skills and knowledge are needed to play this role. And, as for the other higher-order roles, the parents need to be willing and able to play the lower-order roles as well.

As indicated in the previous section, the parents will need to know and understand the information contained in parent handbooks, curriculum guides, and other policy materials. Most important, the parents need to know how the system works.

Even a small elementary school is a bureaucracy and also a part of a much larger organization. Each school and school district has its formal and informal rules and procedures, mores, and a way of doing things. Anyone, in this case, the parents need to know and understand these things in order to be an effective advocate.

While being able to communicate and be supportive, they must be skilled in mediation and conflict resolution. Most family members will need help to enhance these skills. When playing the Advocator Role, it is expected that fully involved parents will:

- help to resolve conflicts, concerns, and problems related to curriculum, programs, and activities
- reinforce the proper enforcement of family and student rights
- monitor the application of school policies and practices
- know and understand school and school district policies
- advocate for curricular and operational policy and procedural reform

Advocator Workshop and Class Topics

Workshops and classes designed to enhance the Advocator Role build on the parents' existing lower-level role skills and knowledge. Some examples of workshop and class subjects are:

- conflict resolution and negotiation
- decision-making skills
- student and parent rights and responsibilities
- school policies and practices
- appealing school actions
- IDEA and Section 504 legislation
- parent rights
- classroom inclusion programs

Other Advocator Role Coaching Best Practices

As with the Advisor Role, the family members will need to be assessed to determine if they have skills and knowledge in such areas as:

- school board policies
- the school's mission and goals

- school regulations
- curriculum
- grade-level learning goals and objectives
- procedures for monitoring student progress
- grading and exam policy
- homework policy
- discipline policy
- attendance and tardy policy
- standardized testing program

When the parents have the prerequisite foundation built by the lower-order roles, best practices like the following can be implemented to enhance the Advocator Role:

Parent rights handbooks. Publish and distribute materials to the families about parent and student rights. For example, parents need to know they have the legal right to:

- look at their child's school records
- a hearing if it is believed that the contents of any record are untrue, inaccurate, or misleading
- insert written explanations with respect to the contents in any record
- expect that the child's records are not released to any individual, agency, or organization without written consent. (There are a few exceptions such as to individuals in the same school who have a legitimate interest or another school where the student is transferring.)
- look at all official school policies
- have a special-needs child placed in an appropriate program
- be present and represent the child at any hearing regarding suspension
- enroll the child in a particular course if she or he is eligible
- expect the school district to adequately supervise and protect the child while being transported in a school bus and in attendance at all school activities

Coaching the Collaborator Parent Partner Role

The goal of the Collaborator Parent Partner Role is to work effectively with the school and community to help with problem-solving, decision-making, and policy development. The term "Collaborator" is used because it expresses the partnership relationship. The Collaborator Role is the highest level role and it builds on all of the other Parent Partner Roles. Realistically, few parents will act as collaborators.

Yet, as the school forms partnerships with the families, it is very important to have representation from all segments of the family population when establishing committees, councils, and planning groups. Being a collaborator requires specific skills and knowledge in such areas as policy formation, decision-making, curriculum development, and so forth. To be involved in the planning and development of family/school partnerships, the collaborators need to understand the Self-Renewing Partnership Model.

When playing the Collaborator Role, it is expected that fully involved parents will:

- participate in family/school partnership planning groups, school improvement and community councils, special projects, and school committees where parents have equal status with professionals and representatives from the community
- help the school take on some of the tougher issues
- assist in reducing educational barriers
- monitor health, library, and cultural services to make sure they are easily accessible to the school and neighborhood
- attend school board meetings when appropriate
- serve on the school board and city council
- be prepared to influence school policy and appeal local school or school system decisions that are questionable or not understood
- participate on committees that focus on issues such as maintaining a safe environment in and around the campus and bus safety, upgrading and beautifying the school building and grounds, and establishing and maintaining high standards and expectations, quality programs, and extracurricular options

Collaborator Workshops and Class Topics

Because this is the highest order Parent Partner Role, the potential workshop and class topics cover a wide range of subjects and issues. Some examples of topics are:

- leadership skills and development
- decision-making and problem-solving
- small group behavior
- school and bus safety
- school violence and discipline
- computer-assisted instruction
  - IDEA and Section 504 legislation

- inclusion of special-needs children in the classroom
  - No Child Left Behind (ESEA) legislation
- curriculum development
- policy formation
- school governance
- school budget
- school effectiveness

Other Collaborator Role Coaching Best Practices

Field trips. Organize family field trips to regular school board meetings; public hearings on such issues as pupil assignment, violence, curriculum change; town council sessions; and district-wide education and parent conferences.

Committee Work

When involving parents in committee work, make sure that meetings are structured and action-oriented. They should be guided by well-planned agendas so they move along swiftly. Do not waste time on trivial matters or issues. The participants need to know and understand the scope and responsibilities of the committee or project. The expected outcome should be clearly stated. The family members must feel their services are wanted and that their comments, suggestions, and recommendations will be thoroughly considered. If necessary, provide a workshop on group decision-making.

Standing advisory committee. Organize a standing advisory group, or committee, of parents, teachers, and staff to make recommendations to the principal on school improvement, restructuring, enhancement, and the use of discretionary funds. If the school is involved with a university as a partner school or professional development school, it is a good idea to also have a higher education representative on the committee.

The groups meet regularly and are called into session when special needs or projects arise. If space is available, the chairperson of the group is provided an office or desk near the principal. The titles for this type of group include: family/school partnership committee, school improvement council, school planning and management team, and similar names.

Ad Hoc committee. If a special issue is facing the school district or school, and if there is a need to develop new policies, a broadly representative parent and community Ad Hoc committee is formed to study the issue and make recommendations. The committee considers such issues as school reorganization, bond proposals, building needs, curriculum changes, smoking, and alcohol and drug abuse, and so forth.

In cooperation with school officials, the group drafts a policy or regulation, which is circulated among the entire student and family bodies for suggestions and comments. After the discussion sessions, the draft is revised and sent to the school board to be considered for adoption.

The Empowering Playground Fence

This chapter began with a story about a remark made to Suzanne Brown, the director of a family/school partnership program in Nashville. When Suzanne came to the inner-city school, drug trafficking was so rampant that dealers drove across the school grounds to get into the neighborhood to sell or to run away from the police. One day, a car roared through the playground with a police car following closely behind. Fortunately, no children were outside playing.

When this happened, a group of parents was meeting with Suzanne. The parents were perplexed and angry. "Those dealers are using the lawn for a racetrack and we do not know what to do," one of the parents exclaimed.

The parents said that there used to be a fence around the playground to protect the children and adults, with gates allowing neighborhood residents access to and from the school grounds. Now the fence was gone and only a few posts remained. "Over the years, the fence was getting torn up and the city did not repair it," said one parent. "The drug dealers pretty much finished it off," added another.

Suzanne had been working with the parents to enhance their Collaborator Role skills. For the past few weeks, they had been studying how to be more involved in school governance and community development. Suzanne had an idea and went to the principal to discuss her strategy. The principal made some suggestions and said she would help in any way she could. When the coordinator met with the parents again, she presented her idea.

"Let's get the city to rebuild the fence," she said. "We will never be able to get them to do that," replied a parent, "Nobody listens to us." "Oh yes they will, if we work together," exclaimed Suzanne. "Let's form a plan."

Suzanne helped the parents to compose a letter to the mayor explaining the problem at the school. They took pictures of the playground and the remaining fence posts and enclosed them with the letter.

The parents were first very excited and then disappointed when the reply from the mayor arrived the next week. The letter thanked the parents for letting him know about the problem and said that he had passed the letter and pictures onto the superintendent of schools. In a few days, a letter arrived from the assistant superintendent for building and grounds, indicating he was concerned about their problem, but that there was no money in the budget for a new fence.

"They ain't going to do nothing," said a dejected parent. "We are not through yet," said Suzanne encouragingly. "I think we need to present our

request to the school board. Maybe if they heard about our problem they would find the money." "I would be scared to do that," responded a parent. "There is nothing to be afraid of. We just need to do it right," said Suzanne.

She said if the parents worked as a group they would have more power and have a better chance to be heard. They talked about communication, conflict resolution, and negotiation. The group decided which parent would call the school board office to see if they could be placed on the next meeting's agenda. When the parent returned, she was very excited. "They said we would be able to speak to the board at their next meeting." "Now we have to get as many parents and teachers to the meeting as possible," commented Suzanne.

The group decided how they would go out into the neighborhood to get people to come to the meeting. The principal agreed to find funds to pay for a school bus to transport the parents to the meeting. The parents met with the school's faculty to see if the faculty members would support their effort. Suzanne explained to the parents the importance of keeping the mayor, superintendent, and assistant superintendent on their side and not alienating them. She helped them write a letter explaining why they had decided to meet with the board.

Finally, the day arrived for the meeting. An excited group of parents gathered at the school and loaded onto the buses. So many parents had decided to attend that two buses were needed. "This is great," exclaimed the principal. "Let's hope this works," thought Suzanne.

The spokesperson for the parent group presented the problem of the playground fence to the school board. The board members asked the parents, principal, coordinator, superintendent, and assistant superintendent many questions and discussed the issue among themselves. The board president said that they would consider their request after they had a chance to get more information from the city. The parents were feeling down as they left the meeting. "Well, at least we tried," said one of the parents. "We learned a lot even if they decide not to get us a fence," said another. The parents all agreed that trying to get the fence was a learning experience, and they felt good about what they had done.

The following week, the principal asked Suzanne to come down to her office. "I just received a call from the assistant superintendent of building and grounds," she bubbled, "They are going to put up a new fence next week."

The school board members, mayor, superintendent, and assistant superintendent attended the dedication for the new fence. The parents had planned the program themselves. When Suzanne spoke, she praised the parents for their good work and courage.

"You did it," Suzanne exclaimed. "Working together, you helped the children, the community, and yourselves." "Now I know what Suzanne means by empowerment," said a parent to the group.

But this great story does not end here. Suzanne worked with the parents and showed them how they had acted as a team, learned to negotiate, and to be assertive. The group continued to meet and found other ways to help the community and the school. The fence is still standing.

SUMMARY

The Coaching Strategy is implemented on the foundation built by the other Partnership Intervention strategies. What best practices are appropriate is determined by the Partnership Intervention Strategy that is being emphasized, which in turn, is determined by the goals and objectives. The goal and objectives are included in the family/school partnership plan.

References

Chrispeels, J. 1988. *Home-School Partnership Planner.* San Diego: San Diego County Office of Education.

Chrispeels, J. 1992. *Home-School Partnership Planner.* San Diego: San Diego County Office of Education.

Comer, J.P. 1980. *School Power: Implications of an Intervention Project.* New York: Macmillan Publishing/The Free Press.

Covey, S.R. 1992. *Principle-Centered Leadership.* New York: Simon and Schuster/ Fireside.

Crew, R. and Dyja, T. 2007. *Only Connect: The Way to Save Our Schools.* New York: Farrar, Straus, and Giroux.

Epstein, J.L. 1987. "Toward a Theory of Family-School Connections: Teacher Practices and Parent Involvement," in *Social Intervention: Potential and Constraints,* K. Hurrelman, F. Kaufmann, and F. Losel, eds. New York: DeGruyter.

Epstein, J.L. 1992. "School and Family Partnerships," in M.C. Alkin ed. *Encyclopedia of Educational Research* (6th ed.). New York: Macmillan, pp. 1,139–1,151.

Epstein, J.L. et al. 2009. *School, Family, and Community Partnerships: Your Handbook for Action* (3rd ed.). Thousand Oaks, CA: Corwin Press.

Henderson, A.T. 1987. *The Evidence Continues to Grow: Parent Involvement Improves Student Achievement.* Columbia, MD: National Committee for Citizens in Education.

Henderson, A.T., Marburger, C.L. and Ooms, T. 1986. *Beyond the Bake Sale: An Educator's Guide To Working With Parents.* Columbia, MD: The National Committee for Citizens in Education.

Henderson, A.T., Mapp, K.L., Johnson, V.R., and Davies, D. 2007. *Beyond the Bake Sale: The Essential Guide to Family-School Partnerships.* New York: The New Press.

Kressley, G. 2008. "Breaking New Ground: Seeding Proven Practices into Proven Programs" in *Handbook of School-Family Partnerships,* S.L. Christenson and A.L. Reschly, Eds. Boston MA: Routledge, (21), p. 3.

References

Kussrow, P.G. 1988. *Community Education Resources Infusion Module for K-12 Instructors.* Boone, NC: North Carolina Center for Community Education.

Lightfoot, S.L. 1978. *Worlds Apart: Relationships Between Families and Schools.* New York: Basic Books.

Lindle, J.C. 1989. "What Do Parents Want from Principals and Teachers?" *Educational Leadership,* 47(2): 12–14.

Lueder, D. C. 1989. "Tennessee Parents Were Invited to Participate and They Did," *Educational Leadership,* 47(2): 15–17.

Rich, D. 1987. *School and Families: Issues and Actions.* Washington, DC: National Education Association.

Rich, D. 1988. *MegaSkills: How Families Can Help Children Succeed in School and Beyond.* Boston, MA: Houghton Mifflin.

Rioux, J.W. and Berla, N. 1993. *Innovations in Parent & Family Involvement.* Princeton Junction, NJ: Eye on Education.

Rutherford, B., ed. 1995. *Creating Family/School Partnerships.* Columbus, OH: National Middle School Association.

Seeley, D.S. 1985. *Education Through Partnership.* Washington, DC: American Enterprise Institute for Public Policy Research.

Seeley, D.S. 1989. "A New Paradigm for Parent Involvement," *Educational Leadership,* 47(2): 46–48.

Index

Breinigsville, PA USA
06 January 2011
252796BV00001B/1/P